THE GREAT NEW ZEALAND SONGBOOK

Autographs

THE GREAT
NEW ZEALAND
SONGBOOK

LAST CENTURY

Tihore Mai — MOANA & THE TRIBE
Give It a Whirl — SPLIT ENZ
Whaling — DD SMASH
Dominion Rd. — THE MUTTON BIRDS
Why Does Love Do This To Me ⟶
                              THE EXPONENTS
~~How Bizz~~ How Bizarre — OMC
Taller Than God — STRAWPEOPLE
April Sun In Cuba — DRAGON
Sinner — NEIL FINN
Break In The ~~Who~~ Weather — JENNY MORRIS
Sitting Inside My Head — SUPERGROOVE
Heavenly Pop Hit — THE CHILLS
Counting the Beat — THE SWINGERS
Nature // THE FOURMYULA
Drive ⇒ BIC RUNGA
Slice of Heaven — DAVE DOBBYN + HERBS
Gutter Black — HELLO SAILOR
Home Again..................... SHIHAD

Venus — THE FEELERS
For Today — NETHERWORLD DANCING TOYS
Better Be Home Soon...... CROWDED HOUSE

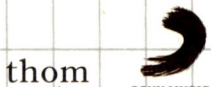

www.thommusic.com

ISBN 978-0-473-14749-5

We gratefully acknowledge permission from Foodstuffs (NZ) Limited and Icon
Images NZ Ltd to use the Mr Four Square image, www.mrfoursquare.co.nz

www.greatnewzealandsongbook.com

The inspiration behind this project came as I walked out of the Vector Arena in Auckland following the amazing Split Enz concert in March 2008. I turned to my son Sam and said, "You've just heard the great New Zealand songbook!" and immediately thought, "I like the way that sounded". I thought about it for a day or two and decided it could be divided into two parts: a selection of The Best New Zealand Music from Last Century and The Best New Zealand Music from This Century.

Very early on in the development process, I was at my in-laws' place. They have spent a lifetime collecting New Zealand art and my mother-in-law Sondra Wigglesworth was showing me a book on Dick Frizzell. From the outset, I wanted this production to encapsulate more than just the music and for reasons I can't explain, I felt it would be great to invite Dick to make an artistic contribution. Dick and I had never met, but he graciously allowed me to visit him in Haumoana to share what I had in mind regarding his involvement. I knew we had made some progress when he said, "Let's see if Jude's got some soup in the pot?" As we talked, I became aware of Dick's deep roots within the New Zealand music industry, his work for a number of record companies 'back in the day' and his design work for Dragon, Radio Hauraki, The Ngaruawahia Music Festival and The Record Warehouse, to name a few. I am grateful to Dick for his enthusiastic participation.

I grew up in Allum Street and my family lived next door to the Lawrys. We all attended Selwyn College in Kohimarama and almost every day, either before or after dinner, I would join the Lawry boys and listen to their current favourite album while playing snooker on their Dad's full-sized table. Lots of Van Morrison, Crosby Stills Nash & Young and Blind Faith (which Mum later broke over her knee). We loved the music, but were equally engaged in the extensive liner notes that came with each LP.

Historically, the music business has had a strong link with great design. Double albums with gatefolds with the most incredible artwork and inner sleeves that told an entire story, along with complete lyrics from every track to read and appreciate; they really were works of art. One thing the music industry has lost over the years are these works of art. So, with these great memories in mind, we invited all the songwriters and artists involved in this project to handwrite their lyrics and provide us with sketches, photos, memorabilia and any anecdotes behind the songs that maybe we weren't aware of.

We were looking for treasure.

We started with Dave as he and I had worked together on his 'Loyal' album back in 1987 - he submitted 'Welcome Home' and this was the first spread to be completed.

Dave is one of just five artists who feature more than once, along with Bic, Don, Neil and Tim. Speaking of Bic, I briefed her and Boh at a café in West Hollywood. I offered a Pinky bar to the sister who submitted her material first (Boh won). We chatted to Brooke over lunch in Castle Hill, Evermore and Phil Judd were in Melbourne and Jenny Morris, Todd Hunter and Margaret Urlich in Sydney. Moana met with us in a café in Ponsonby Road having just given birth to her baby girl, Manawa, the previous week! Every encounter with every artist has been a highlight and this entire production has been such a joy.

I want to express my very sincere appreciation to all the great New Zealand songwriters and artists who have enthusiastically shared their treasure with us. It is my great privilege to have collaborated with you all, to now present The Great New Zealand Songbook.

Murray Thom

SYDNEY HIRINI MELBOURNE (TUHOE)
1949 - 2003

For many years, I've opened my live sets with this song. There's something very powerful about its simplicity. It conveys a sense of wairua, yet is grounding.

This song reinforces our roots, identity and our connections to Papatuanuku. This is really important especially when we are in foreign lands

There is a simple truth in this waiata that rises above language + culture. It's the reason we perform this song despite not writing it ourselves.

Hirini Melbourne (Tuhoe) was my lecturer at Waikato University.) hardly turned up to class and a couple of times when I did, HE was AWOL! But he still gave me an A which says nothing about my intelligence, more about him being so generous.

Tihore mai pays homage to the elements. A prolific songwriter, Hirini began composing as a way to teach his children te Reo. He is ICONIC in te AO MAORI for his waiata

KA RAWE!!

Moana

Moana & the Trib'e

Inspired by a traditional waiata
Written by Hirini Melbourne
Recorded by Moana & the Moahunters
still performed by Moana & the tribe
...and tamariki throughout the motu!!

Tihore Mai

Tihore mai te rangi
Tihore mai
Mao mao mao te ua
Whiti mai te rā

E rere kōtare
ki runga pūwharawhara
Rūrū parirau
Kai mate i te ua

E rere e noke
Mai tō pokorua
Kai kī i te wai
Kai mate i te ua

E...I...E
Whiti mai te ra

Clear the skies
Cease the rains
Let the sun shine through
Fly Kingfisher onto
the pūwharawhara tree
Ruffle your feathers
Lest you catch a chill
Worm, wriggle out of your burrow
lest it fills with water
and you drown

E...I...E
Let the sun shine

Dave Dobbyn

MANGAWHAI HEADS
NORTHLAND

It was a street protest against racism in Christchurch that sparked 'Welcome Home'. I wrote it at Mangawhai Heads, where it couldn't be more peaceful or welcoming.

As occasional songs go, it's been a grand surprise to me to see people take to it so open-heartedly. It's a great ice-breaker in a waiata sense and for my band it's a song that has a point of difference every time we play, so it has a whole life of its own.

What more could a songwriter ask for?

DD

Welcome Home by Dave Dobbyn

Tonight I am feeling for you
Under the state of a strange land
You have sacrificed much to be here
There for the grace as I offer my hand
Welcome Home, I bid you welcome, we bid you welcome
Welcome Home from the bottom of my heart

Out here on the edge empire is fading by the day
And the world is so weary in war
Maybe we'll find that new way
Welcome Home, you see I made a space for you now
Welcome Home from the bottom of our hearts
Keep it coming now, Keep it coming now
You'll find most of us here with our hearts wide open
Keep it coming now, Keep it coming now, Keep it coming now

There's a woman with her hands trembling - haere mae
And she sings with a mountain's memory - haere mae
There's a cloud the full length of these isles
Just playing chase with the sun
And it's black and it's white and it's wild
And all the colours are one

So Welcome Home, I bid you Welcome, We bid you Welcome
Welcome Home, see I made a space for you now
Welcome Home from the bottom of our hearts
From the Bottom of our hearts

i would give
the world to
tell your story,
'cause I know
that you called
me, I know that
you've called me

68

3. Be Thou my_ bat-tle-shield,_ sword for the fight; Be
4. Rich -es I_ heed not, nor_ man's emp-ty praise; Thou
5. High King of_ hea - ven, af-ter vic -tor -y won, May

So ... the whole thing is...

brookefraser

songbook

Be Thou my_ vi - sion, O_ Lord of my heart; Nau
the places that used to fit me cannot hold the things I've yearned
Be Thou my SLANE bat-tle-shield, sword for the fight;

BROOKE FRASER

Is 43: 1. Be
1-2 2. Be

"Trust in the Lord with all your heart and lean not
on your own understanding. In all your ways
acknowledge him and he will make your paths straight."
- Proverbs 3:5-6

speaking de...
worthy of the...
When we...
when I do...
reputation...
we're God's...
all names...
stop making ex...

"Don't let...
Paul wrote...
Paul is talking...
have condesce...
the Church...
Paul hints tha...
get away with...
older, "wiser"

In fact, the sec...
clearly that w...
compromise.
rest of the fa...

"Don't let anyo...
but set an ex...
love, in faith a...

Jesus is not a...
and Lord of Lo...

Blessings,

brook

ARITHMETIC

I've been staring at the sky tonight
Marvelling and passing time
Wondering what to do with daylight
Until I can make you mine
You are the one I want

I've been thinking of changing my mind
It never stays the same for long
But, of all the things I know for sure,
You're the only certain one
You are the one I want

I've been counting up all my wrongs
One "sorry" for each star
See I'd apologise my way to you
If the heavens stretched that far
You are the one I want

I won't find what I am looking for
If I only "see" by keeping score
'Cause I know now you are so much more
than arithmetic

'Cause if I add, if I subtract
If I give it all, try to take some back
I've forgotten the freedom that comes from the fact
That you are the sum
So you are the one I want

When the years are showing on my face
And my strongest days are gone
When my heart and flesh depart this place
From a life that sung your song:

You'll still be the one I want
You'll still be the one I want
You'll still be the one I want
You'll still be the one I want.

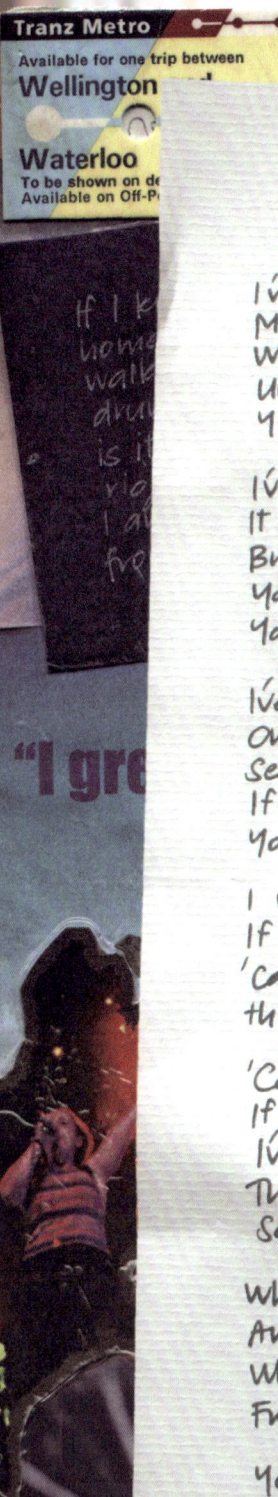

the exponents

Why Does

V1: I walked out - You left me
You know I'm hurting for you
It seems now, that it's over
And there is nothing I can do.

CH: I don't know - woe oh oh
Why does love do this to me
I don't know. I don't know.

V2: Jackie came - she went away
Deep in the valley, I kissed her that day
It seems I'm thinkin' of you
But I'm still thinkin' about myself....

CH: I don't know - oh - woe - oh
Why does love do this to me?
I don't know - woah woah oh
Why does love do this to me?
I don't know, I don't know!

Guitars... Guitars... egg shaker
+ more guitars

V3: I miss you - you know that
But when I see you sometimes
I'm cut up - yeah + I'm broken
+ There am I.. asking you how you are
Jackie came - she went away
Deep in the valley, I kissed her that day
It seems I'm thinking of you...
But I'm still thinking of someone else

CH: I don't know - Why does love do this to me?
...... + out.......

Jordan Luck on way to New Zealand
A very early navigator

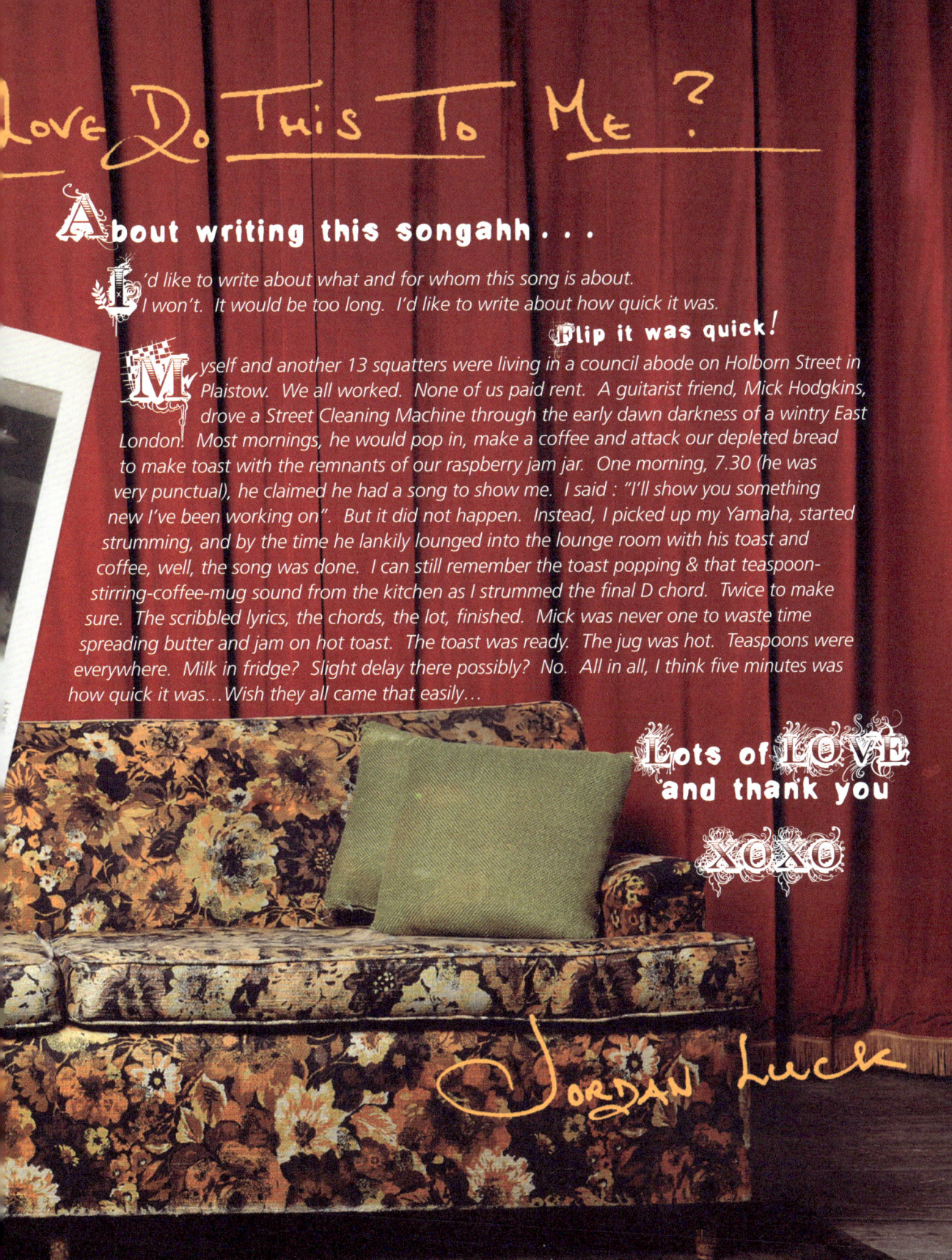

Love Do This To Me?

About writing this songahh . . .

I'd like to write about what and for whom this song is about. I won't. It would be too long. I'd like to write about how quick it was.

Flip it was quick!

Myself and another 13 squatters were living in a council abode on Holborn Street in Plaistow. We all worked. None of us paid rent. A guitarist friend, Mick Hodgkins, drove a Street Cleaning Machine through the early dawn darkness of a wintry East London! Most mornings, he would pop in, make a coffee and attack our depleted bread to make toast with the remnants of our raspberry jam jar. One morning, 7.30 (he was very punctual), he claimed he had a song to show me. I said : "I'll show you something new I've been working on". But it did not happen. Instead, I picked up my Yamaha, started strumming, and by the time he lankily lounged into the lounge room with his toast and coffee, well, the song was done. I can still remember the toast popping & that teaspoon-stirring-coffee-mug sound from the kitchen as I strummed the final D chord. Twice to make sure. The scribbled lyrics, the chords, the lot, finished. Mick was never one to waste time spreading butter and jam on hot toast. The toast was ready. The jug was hot. Teaspoons were everywhere. Milk in fridge? Slight delay there possibly? No. All in all, I think five minutes was how quick it was…Wish they all came that easily…

Lots of LOVE
and thank you
XOXO

Jordan Luck

...But it's getting better now
He found it in him to forgive
He walked the city
And he found a place to live
In a halfway house
Halfway down Dominion Road...

DOMINION RD

234   236

Dominion Road

Performed by: The Mutton Birds (Ross Burge,
David Long, Alan Gregg and Don McGlashan)

The band hadn't been going long, and most of
my songs seemed to be coming out slow and
dark. I didn't know what sort of people
(if any) would come to our gigs, but I was
hoping that whoever they were, they'd jump
up and down and spill their drinks on each other,
rather than stroke their chins and say "hmmm,
interesting", so I was looking for a way to get
more energy into things. I saw this guy in
the street, and I wanted to tell his story in a song.
He looked like Fate had thrown him some bad
passes - but he seemed to have a spark of
redemption in him. It turned into a story
of a life unravelling, and then starting to come
together again. And it was upbeat + loud.

The song went through phases - sometimes easy
to play, sometimes hard. I was always proud
of the way we did it. Oh, and people
did jump up and down and spill their drinks.

NO ORDINARY THING WILL ALWAYS HAVE AN ESOTERIC NATURE TO ME.
WHEN I START SINGING THIS SONG I STILL GET THE SAME CHILL UP MY
SPINE AS I DID WHEN LONG AGO I FIRST COMBINED TWO LYRICAL PHRASES
FROM TWO VERY DIFFERENT SONGS.
"WAS THIS TO SHOW YOU" AND "I WOULD NOT FAIL YOU".
I DON'T KNOW WHY NECESSARILY.
MAYBE IT'S THE NOTION THAT THOSE LYRICS CONJURE UP A SENSE OF
BEING MONITORED.   WHATEVER IT IS, IT STIRS ME.
ONE THING I RECALL
WHEN I WROTE IT IS
LOOKING UP AT THE
CONSTELLATION OF ORION.
PERHAPS THAT'S WHY THE SONG UNFOLDS INTO
SOMETHING QUITE INFINITE AND EERIE AND
INVOKES SOME WEIRD GRAVITAS.
IT HAD AN AMORPHOUS BIRTH
AND IT SEEMS TO HAVE
MAINTAINED A MYSTIQUE.

EVERY TIME WE PLAY IT
I THINK I MIGHT HAVE IT NAILED
THEN I GET THROWN OFF THE SCENT AND INTO A DIFFERENT MEANING
CERTAINLY DIFFERENT LAYERS KEEP REVEALING THEMSELVES.
INDEED, THE FACT THAT SOME FOLK GET WHATEVER THEY DO FROM THE MUSIC
AS IMMEDIATELY AS THEY DO OCCURS TO ME AS A SOURCE OF SOMETHING
BOTH EXTRAORDINARY AND FRUSTRATING.

EITHER WAY, I'M SURE THIS MANTRA WILL REVEAL ITSELF TO ME HOWEVER IT
CHOOSES AND MAYBE I'LL EVENTUALLY BE CONTENT JUST TO HAVE WRITTEN IT

OR PERHAPS OTHERS MAY START HEARING LAYERS TOO.   ULTIMATELY IT FEELS
LIKE AN AFFIRMATION EVERY TIME AND I LOVE THAT.

JASON

No Ordinary Thing - Opshop

VERSE 1:

Em   G
WAS this to show you

C   Am
I would not FAIL you

Em   G
WaS that thE reASon you WE're

C   Am
LOOK.in' back

      Em   G
So I'm TRUST.in' in EXIST.ence

      C   Am
I'm ThRUST.IN' on MOMENT.tum

Em   G
I don't wanna SEE these THrEads of

C   Am
LOVE COmE

Not ever again.
               C
      G   C G
No, not EVER AGAIN. No

Em   G
I kNOW. it's NOt W.orking

                      Am
KNOW.ledge wilL captURE comfort

one day
    Em   G
Our worlds WILL be worth more than

C   Am
living once IN THIS LIFE.time

    Em   G
If WE could liberate today

         C   Am
We COULD alleviate tomorrow

    Em   G
But no one can REACH the light

switch

   C   Am
No one can reach the LIGHT switch,

   C G
they say

Amaj   C   G
No, that's what they say... No

Em   C
My LOVE

               G   D
This IS. no ordinary thing, my love

         Em
My LOVE, my love

             G
This IS. no ordinary thing

D   A
No, THIS IS NO ordinary thing

VERSE 2:

I'm naked, I'm naked in this AFTER.
LIFE.

I was fallin', I was fallin' from the
GREATest highs

If everything, if everyTHING Should
come to PASS.

Tell me when are YOU comin' home
to stay

When ARE you comin' home TO
STAY.

Again to stay
Again'

(CHORUS)

                     D
We were COMPROMISE.d

                A
By our own hearts

             D   A
Jealous seas couldn't keep us apart

           D
I WANTed to touch YOU.

                   A
But we stop when we start

              D
I WANTed to hold you, hold YOU,

                   Em
But here we are, Here WE ARE

No, this WAS NO ordinary THING.

Am7
I know it's late now
                    G
I know I ought to
  Fmaj7
ride in your car now
     Am7
but please don't drop
    Fmaj7
My head's so heavy
Am7   G
could this be all a
     Fmaj7
promise me maybes
Am7   G
x say things you don...
     Fmaj7

Am7
Keep my heart turning
        Fmaj7   G
on axles around you
  Am7   G
keep our love burning
  Fmaj7
just like it used to
Am7   G
Now just for us,
        Fmaj7
they could play our favourit...
Am7   G
Let's not discuss
             Fmaj7
all these things we can...

Rung 9   capo 5th fret

go

me home.

dream?

mean.

               $Fmaj^7$ G Am^7

Rain fall from concrete - coloured skies

No boy don't speak now, you just

Drive. Drive,

Drive, speed me through

make me feel alive, alive,

When I ride with you.

Let rain fall from concrete - coloured skies

No boy don't speak now, you just drive,

Drive, drive

speed me through, make me feel alive

Alive, when I ride with you.

Rain fall from concrete - coloured skies,

No boy don't speak now, you just drive.

do

tune

ndo.

"Sitting Inside My Head" – SUPERGROOVE

I walk around this town as buildings close & windows are boarded;
I think about you.....
When I hear a door slam in the wind and the glass on the mat says 'welcome';
I think about you....

> Sitting inside my head, laughing at what I said,
> Come on baby let's have another toast.
> You might think I'm dense, laughing at my expense,
> Fill the cup let's wash away the ghost.

In this ghost town where we live there's a wanted poster of you on
every corner; she keeps asking me 'who's that?' and 'what's her name?'
But I choke on every letter, as the glass flies off the table;
I keep telling her I ain't the one to blame.

> Sitting inside my head....

I left when I was gone; I didn't feel a thing; I never dreamt you'd
haunt me this long after.
But the buildings crumble down, as I run from the town;
I hear you breathe and I listen to your laughter.

> Sitting inside my head....

I walk around this town as buildings close & windows are boarded;
I think about you...
When I hear a door slam in the wind and the glass on the mat says 'welcome';
I think about you....

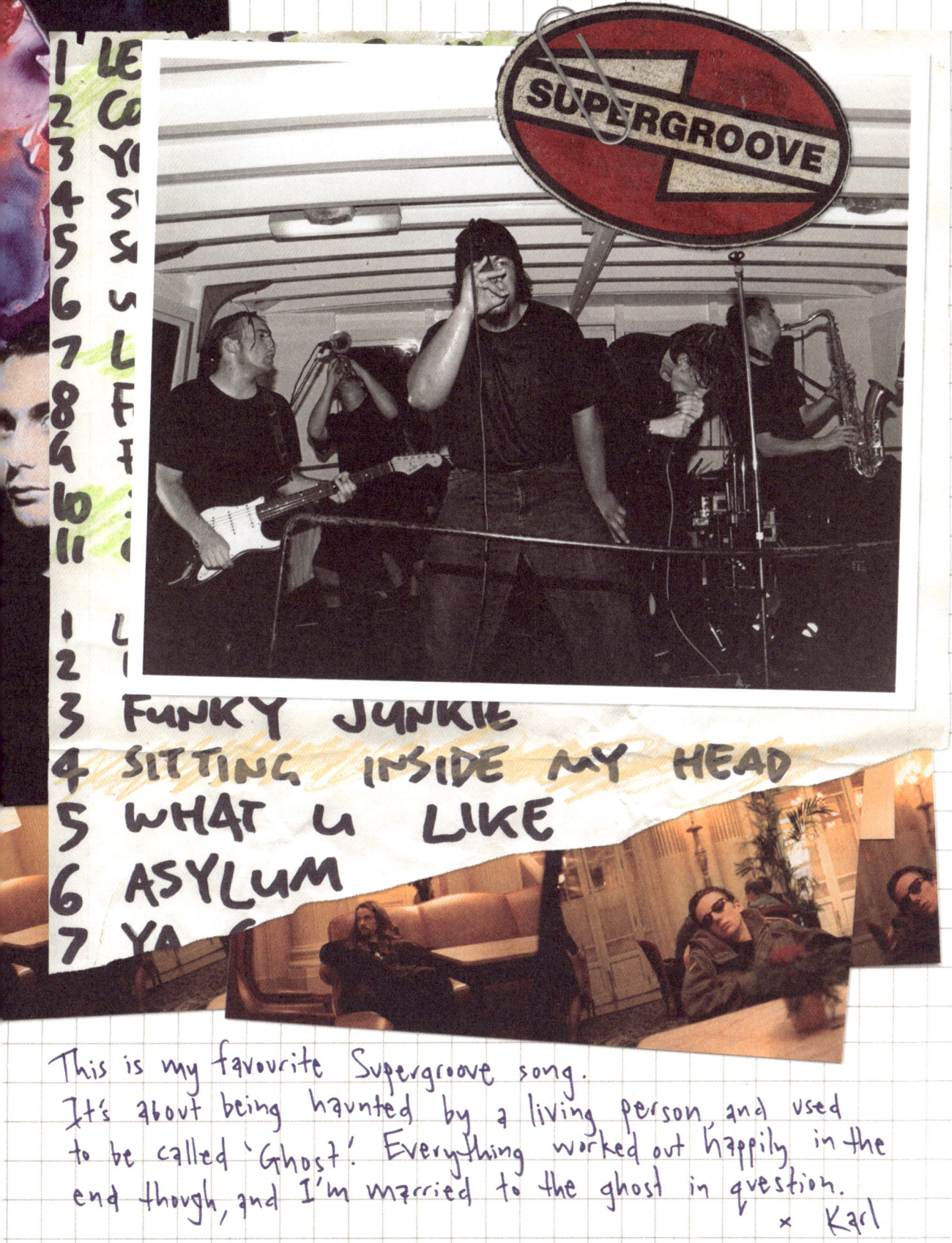

1 LE
2 CO
3 YO
4 SI
5 SK
6 U
7 U
8 F
9 F
10 M
11

1
2
3 FUNKY JUNKIE
4 SITTING INSIDE MY HEAD
5 WHAT U LIKE
6 ASYLUM
7 YA

This is my favourite Supergroove song.
It's about being haunted by a living person and used
to be called 'Ghost'. Everything worked out happily in the
end though, and I'm married to the ghost in question.
x Karl

I was working with Marius De Vries
he has all sorts of amazing loops &
samples in his "fridge." He left me
with the guitar,
piano & vibraslap
and I wrote
the song to
this backing
strumming my
acoustic along &
remembering the
time I snuck out
my bedroom window
when I was about
8 years old
It was a full
moon and
I took off all my
clothes and danced around the
back lawn. It was a glorious
feeling and I highly recommend it

Neil Finn

See it anyone got my eyes, got my face
sing it everyone got my nose, got my blood
conscience plays upon me now
safe until my luck runs out
cuckoos call, pendulum swings
I thought you knew everything
lift my hands, make the cross
sinner I have never learned
beginner I cannot return
forever I must walk this earth
like some forgotten soldier
these things I should keep to myself
but I feel somehow strangely compelled
under moonlight I stood wild & naked
felt no shame just my spirit awakened

SINNER

fireball drop from the sky
all my dreams have come to pass
where's my faith - is it lost?
can't see it till I cast it off
sinner there is no such thing
beginner I have learned to sing
forever I must walk this earth
like some forgotten soldier
today I am still disconnected
to the face that I saw in the clouds
and the closest i get to contentment
is when all of the barriers come dow

Verse 1 ... you may not remember me , I am the girl with the tear
in her eye, tear in her eye
I never expected a call from you , but thinking about
it now, I guess I did , I guess I did

Chorus . Cos I have all these dreams in my head
of you and I together walking in eachother's arms
if only I could tell you how I feel
then I wouldn't have to sit and think about losing you

Verse 2 . the moon is up and I'm shaking my head
it's been another day of missing you
of missing you
and on this island there's the two of us
Sinking in the sand of our desperate love
our desperate love ...

     Chorus

bridge . If you could see, my heart is bleeding
i'll stay, here now, and wait for you to show

     chorus again

Cos it's just a dream, I have in my head
it makes me quite sad, that it's unrequited lo...
       Boohoo!!

VANUATU
23 FEB

AIR MAIL
FIRST CLASS MAIL
VANUATU

I was in Vanuatu when I wrote
Dreams in my head. I'd met a beautiful
woman and was completely infatuated with her
and I missed her, so I wrote the song on
this beautiful island. It was hot and I swam lots but I walked around with
my guitar and my best friend Justin and the words + melody kept arriving
so we'd have to stop while I wrote ....

When I finished the song I got drunk next to the sea, and passed out.
I was blissfully happy but very sad because I thought I'd never see her again.
I did see her again ....

The moral to this story is write love songs to people and show them
and they fall in love with you. hahaha!

Anika X

Dreams In My Head
Anika Moa
- Key of Am7 -

And so I stand and the sound goes straight through my
and I'm growing in stages – and have
and free... Aaahh...
It's a heavenly

Not long after The Chills released our single, 'Heavenly Pop Hit', I spoke about the creativ... to a class at one of Dunedin's more established high schools. I was asked to nam... It wasn't until some time afterwards that I realised that I was expected t... What a load of lightweight rubbish!' — that was what was expected by all those brigh... again and again and again... and if one didn't sound like that! Well! You were just so outdate... honesty and energy in so many other types of musical expression — and I still do. — urgent need to rise above the squalor and the dull-minded, futureless attitude of th... of humanity — our need to discover the sublime amongst the generally sordi... and those who record our music to understand that melodies don't necessari... and that is what I want to hear driving my songs, live or on record, whether they'r... So the potential of 'Heavenly Pop Hit' was never fully realised in the studio bu... to smash into the faces of the deliberately hard and cynical. MARTIN PHILLIPPS

...oody I'm so bloated up happy I could throw things around me
...een for ages Just singing, and floating
...pop hit

if anyone
wants it

The Chills

...rocess and the outcome
...e worst song I had ever written
...ave said "Oh, 'Heavenly Pop Hit'!
...oung kids who listened to Nirvana's "Nevermind" album
...felt sorry for their lack of insight and ability to recognise
...main proud that I wrote this song for it caught something of the
...asses and to show something of that most wonderful aspect
...hich is our lot. It has always been difficult to get musicians
...rean "pop". I was initially inspired by the energy, fun and fury of "punk"
...pbeat or whether they are slow, sad and more like ballads.
...eaknesses and all, my song is still a strengthened cream-pie.

How Bizarre

Pauly Fuemana

Brother Peles in the back
Sweet Sina in the front
Cruising down the freeway
in the hot, hot sun
Suddenly red, blue lights
flash us from behind
Loud voice booming

Please step out on to the line.
Pele Preach Word of comfort
Sina Just hides her eyes
Police man taps his shades
"is that a chevy 69?"
How bizarre
How bizarre
How bizarre

Destination
as we pull in
a freshly
reveals a smile
theres elephants
lions
Pele speak
Sister Sina
How b
oooh
its making
everytime I
its in mc
Ring master
says the elephants
People jump
the clowns have
TV news
theres chopper

unknown
or some gas
asted Poster
rom the Pack
and acrobats,
snakes, monkey
righteous
says funky
zarre
baby,
me crazy,
ook around
face
steps out
hants left town,
and jive
stuck around
and cameras
n the sky

Marines, Police, reporters
Ask where, for and ~~why~~ why
Pele yells we're out of here
Siha says right on
we're making moves,
starting grooves
before ~~us knew~~ they knew
we were gone
Jump into the chevy
head for big lights
g want to know the rest
hey) Buy the rights.

Angelo Fuemana
aged 11

Angelo was born the year
"How Bizarre" went number 1 on U.S radio.
Took me round the world
but nothing could replace the love.

liam finn

BETTER TO BE

Better to be
Looking for an answer
Out in the sea
Than under the bed
I'll probably
Just leave it to the morning
My energy
Is already spent
Bottle it up Bottle it up

Better to be
Bigger than the other
Heart on your sleeve
And hat on your head
I want to see
You playing with your shadow
Hypnotise me
With every step
Falling asleep
While sitting at the doctor
I don't believe
A thing that he said
Ordinary
People, like i told you
Are following
Me everywhere

Bottle it up Bottle it up

Girl you seemed so nice
But I'll be gone by morning time
Baby, baby i'll be gone
Fooled me once or twice
But the boy inside can't unwind
Maybe, maybe i'll go home

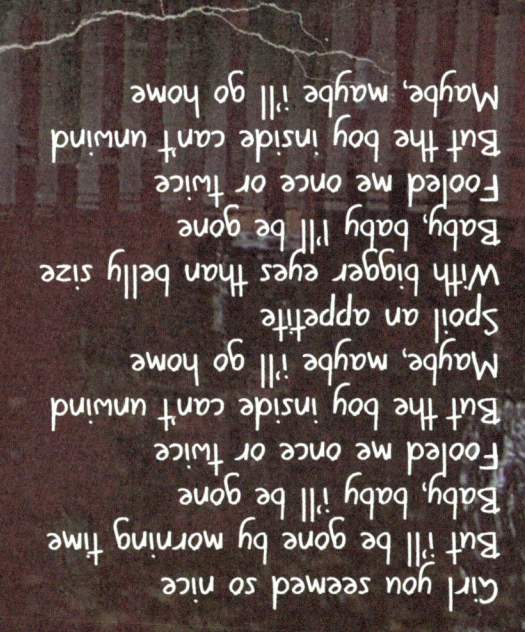

Maybe, maybe i'll go home
But the boy inside can't unwind
Fooled me once or twice
Baby, baby i'll be gone
With bigger eyes than belly size
Spoil an appetite
Maybe, maybe i'll go home
But the boy inside can't unwind
Fooled me once or twice
Baby, baby i'll be gone
But i'll be gone by morning time
Girl you seemed so nice

I was playing in Australia seven nights a week & writing in
the early hours. This song started life on a beer coaster as a
chorus. My fiancée & I wrote love letters daily across the pond.
It was a desperate time for me & touring was hard & brutal.
The idea of the reluctant whaler seemed so right.
I imagined he was traumatized by his job and his hope
    lay in the arms of his love. When I got back home
                to tour and write for the
                Optimist. I finished the lyrics
                on the shores of
                    Lake Okataina.

Whaling

by Dave Dobbyn

Sing bravo bravo, you're a brave brave man
I know it's just bravado, you never sink cos you swim
And when your ship can't handle the heavier seas
Your spirits will get you thru, no down on bended knees
You sing 'save me, save me, save me from myself'
I'm the first to get trigger happy. The first to think
                            of my own health

I remember playing the whole song to my girl with glee
In a cabin with a view of the lake. We were the
only guests in the lodge that time. It was a
perfect way to bring a song home.

Cos I'm whaling out on the green, I'll never get used to the sea

wanted to be

Whaling - manning my harpoon - not where I
Whaling - I feel like Jonah - never meaning you no harm
Whaling - Next port of call,
back in my sweet baby's arms
In a room, close,
savouring our love
while we got rest
& recreation

RADIO HAURAKI

Presents

LIVE IN CONCERT

DRAGON
ACT I and SPACE WAITZ

ENTER THE DRAGON

DRAGON ARE A DISTINCTIVELY AUCKLAND ROCK AND ROLL BAND. THEY FORMED OVER TWO YEARS AGO THE MEMBERS COMING FROM...

THE GREAT NGARUAWAHIA MUSIC FESTIVAL 1973

THREE GREAT DAYS OF MUSIC
OVERSEAS AND LOCAL ARTISTS
ROCK, COUNTRY JAZZ & FOLK
ON 6, 7, 8 JANUARY 12 HOURS EACH DAY
Full camping facilities   Fresh daily provisions
Fresh water, telephones   Shower and toilet facilities
Children's playground   24 hour security and safety
and creche   supervision
First aid post   Riverside site
Follow the signs to Ngaruawahia
GO TO IT

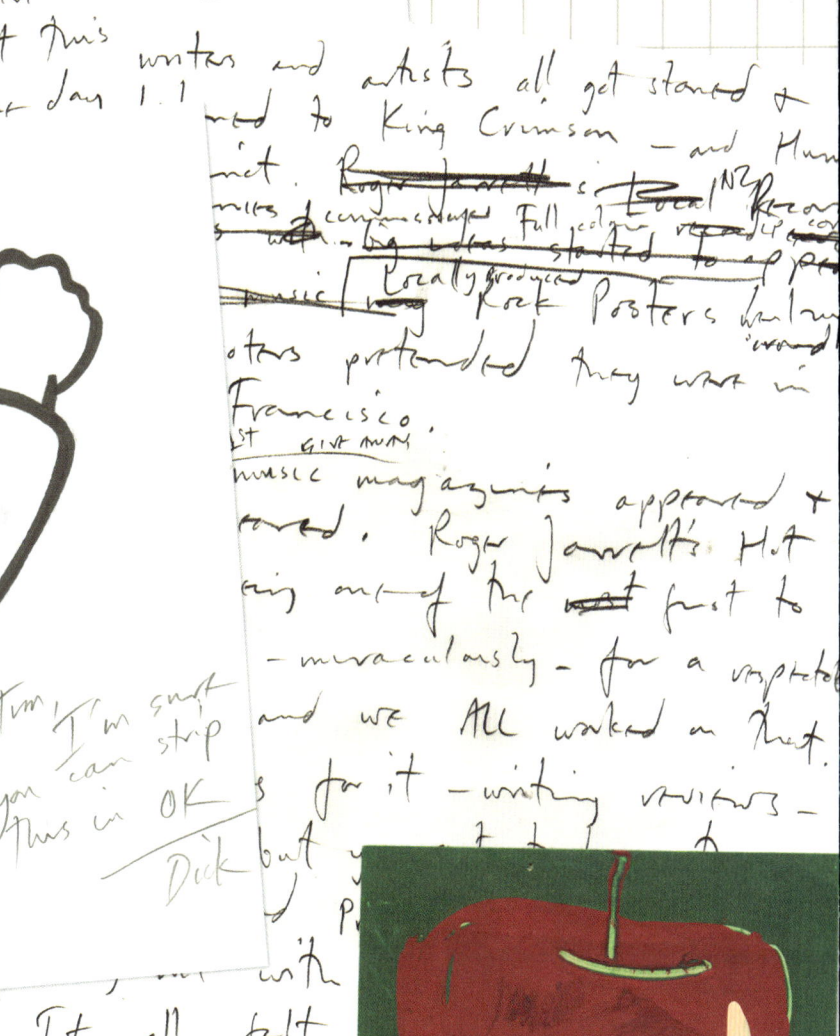

THE STARS FLOW RIGH...
...S ME WHAT I WILL...
...A GONNA FIND

jenny morris
break in the weather

Break In The Weather
(Jenny Morris,
Tam Morris)

VS The cold in your eyes
goes up & down my spine
a vision of a man
that borders on divine
You've got a presence
That spans the great divide
Pierces through the safety shield
To the quiet cave inside

CHOR-ars
I need a break in the weather
Trying to take a breath
Trying to take a little holiday
I need a break in the weather
Trying to take a little breath
for the very first time
Where are we goin'
and what are we going to do
you've got to live a little, love a little
& give a little too
You've got a look you know it
How long have I got, before you roll it
you're the wild that's in my mind
you are the one I need to know

ha Chor-ars

Bubba bubba dups

Tam and I at our house at 28 Hunter Street, Hamilton

...) FOR THE VERY EAST TIME

...rics for "Break in the Weather"

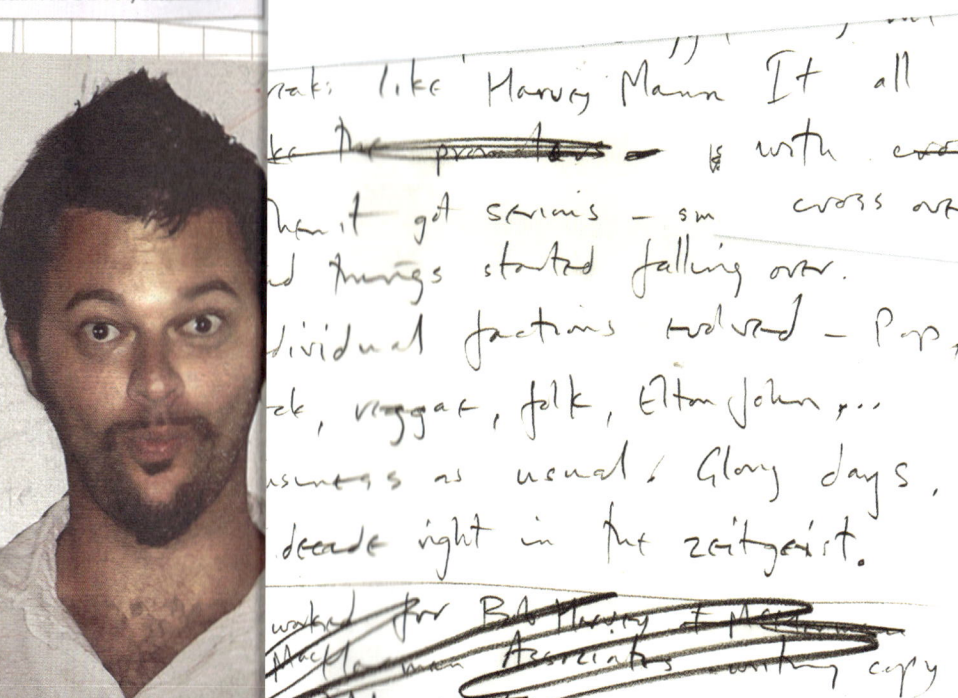

'Back in the day...' where did that come
from? Seems to fit this writers and artists all got stoned &
Rock in the day I.I ...ned to King Crimson — and ...

...ters pretended they went in
...Francisco.

...music magazines appeared &
...eared. Roger Jarrett's H.T
...ing one of the ...first to
...miraculously — for a ...
...and we ALL worked on that.
...s for it — writing reviews —

Tim,
I'm sure
you can strip
this in OK
Dick

...it got serious — sm   cross over.
...things started falling over.
...dividual factions evolved — Pop,
...ck, reggae, folk, Elton John...
...siness as usual. Glory days,
...decade right in the zeitgeist.

...worked for Bob Harvey of the
...Mackenzie-man Associates copy
EMI

Dick Frizzell
is out on his own.
Phone BSY 8.9.133
for creative illustration

Girl you've got me singing with some melody

You're always on my mind

This is what you do to me

Girl you've got me singing with some harmony

Forever you're my queen

and baby girl I'm your king

ALWAYS ON MY MIND

I wrote the song that would become "Break in the Weather" when I was 19. I didn't have a title.

This is the song that was/is most special to me. Having a talented brother who wrote this at such a young age is very special & I've never taken it for granted...

If it was about anything tangible at all it was a mystical song about finding your one true love, having found them before in many past lives. Or something.

The acoustic guitar was my writing tool of choice at the time and I had blundered into these 2 chords which I found out later were major 7ths. Em7 to Am7, I think.

in fact what I DID do was take it to Sly & Robbie, my favourite rhythm section, and let them loose on it. They loved it too.

Anyway I was around at Jenny's place one day and played it to her. She liked it and asked if I would mind if she used it. Did I mind? Hell no.

Jenny adapted the lyrics and added an awesome middle eight which took the song to another level altogether. What was retained from the original were the lines "where are we going?

and what are we gonna do?" as well as the tune, including the breathless chorus, which I think Jen will tell you is one of the things that grabbed her most.

It became the highest-charting song I had — everywhere — and the video, which was directed by Andrew Dominic (Chopper, The Assassination of Jesse James by the Coward Robert Ford) remains my favourite too.

I'm so proud to be associated with that song forever more. I still love it and I think Jenny and the producer Nick Launey, not to mention my childhood heroes Sly and Robbie, did an awesome job. It hits a perfect balance between funkiness and quirky pop hookiness.

I don't think I've ever thanked Jenny properly for embellishing the song and sharing it with the world. So ... thanks Jen. That song changed the course of my life.

As I said, special.

Tam Morris

Jenny Morris

I was painted for the Archibald Prize (Biggest Art comp. in Oz) where artists paint portraits of celebrities. Tam did this artwork of himself posing like me (cheeky bastard).

MY DELIRIUM

Late night, waiting by the phone
~~tonight~~ tonight, waiting for an answer
heartbeat, drumming double time
I need one more chance to be near you.

Still hanging on (for what)
can't operate (fired up)
I wont eat and I wont sleep for you yeah
no rest til I (get through)
Coz I'm holding out (for you)
am I the only one who's insane

Hey! You're playing with my delirium
and the longer I wait the harder I'm gonna fall
Stop! Playing with my delirium
Coz i'm outta my head and outta my self control

Still here in this quiet room
deep in delusion sending me over
Outside watch the world go by
Inside time stands still as I wonder

Still hanging on (for what)
can't operate (fired up)
I won't eat and I won't sleep for you yeah
no rest till I (get through)
Coz i'm holding out (for you)
am I the only one who's insane

Hey! You're playing with my delirium
and the longer I wait the harder I'm gonna fall
Stop! Playing with my delirium
Coz I'm outta my head and outta my
                              self control)

LADYHAWKE

PIP BROWN

My delirium is a song I wrote when I first
arrived in London in 2007.
I was only visiting for a couple of months to
write my album, but it was my first time there
and I didn't know a single person. ~~████~~
I hadn't slept for a couple of nights due to really
bad jet lag, and I was sort of running on some kind of
weird delirium, which was the main inspiration for the
song. I was also really homesick!

I grew up in a town called Masterton, about an hour and
a half north of Wellington.
I went to St. Patricks primary school and Chanel college.
I then moved to wellington when I was 18 and went to
the school of design.
I'd been in bands since I was young, and it was always
something I put to the front of my mind. Most of the time
more-so than school or uni.
I'm glad I'm a New Zealander. Growing up in New Zealand
gives you a massive appreciation and awareness of the rest
of the world. There is always a thirst to travel, and explore,
and see in person, all the things we see as kids, in books or
on television.
A lot of people in larger countries have so much more at
their own doorsteps that it's easier to ignore the fact that
smaller countries exist!
I love travelling the world, and playing my songs to lots of
different people from all corners of the globe. But I also love
that I have New Zealand to ~~██~~ come home to.

Remember those kiwifruit stuffed
toys... my sister had one. We
aquired at this bee place that
sells honey .... somewhere on the
way to taupo from masterton.
I used to love stopping there and
tasting all the honey! →

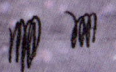

FOR TODAY can best be described as a happy mongrel of a song, where the whole ended up being more than the sum of its parts...

▼ ▼ ▼

Nick writes the chorus and some initial verses. The band starts working it up during a Dunedin heatwave.

Malcolm has a different idea for the verses and scribbles down the lyric (about his girlfriend who's shifted up to Wellington) 20 minutes before the next practice.

↓ ↓ ↓ ↓ ↓

The NDT rhythm section (Burt + Graham) apply the time honoured tradition where white guys try to play with a black feel + come up somewhere in between.

We start rehearsals for the 1984 Orientation tour with 17 year old Annie Crummer, Kim Willoughby and Auckland horns the Newton Hoons. After our first long, hot day's work things stall on the new tune.

- Nick and Tex head out to buy beer and fish n chips leaving the others to have another crack at the song.
- By the time they return Annie has had an 'idea' to the bridge.
- BIG SMILES, COLD BEER & FISH N CHIPS ALL ROUND.

Nick and the Newton Hoons come up with a chart merging their 'flash licks' and the more 'trad NDT ' horn approach.

Nigel Stone is brought on board to produce the first NDT album. He introduces Ross Burge + Rob Wynch who help bring FOR TODAY'S groove to life. Annie delivers her wonderful vocal part.

Brent Hanson offers to make the video. He wants to shoot it on the Wellington/Picton ferry. To this day he doesn't know the band nearly misses the return leg (the bit being filmed) after lunchtime jugs in Picton + had to jump onto the car ramp...

Combined effort is released and to everyone's bewilderment NZ RADIO & TV pick it up.

For Today

Malcolm Black & Nick Sampson
NETHERWORLD DANCING TOYS

If you'd told me, this time last year
That I would feel like I do now, well
I wouldn't have believed you

It's not just a question, of my being alone
The truth is I like my own company best
If the truth is to be known

I didn't realise, babe, just how much I cared
But all I want to do is to be with you
And everything else seems unimportant compared

For Today I'll remember your smile
For Today I'll remember your smile...

It's been a hot summer now
Things the way they should be
But there's a hole, in my well being

So big now, you could drive a truck right through
I think you should them that you are the one
Who could probably fill it for good...

For Today I'll remember your smile
For Today I'll remember your smile...

Today it gets played at footy games,
schools, day-care centres, parties, weddings
and funerals. We feel honoured.
Who'd have thought eh!

SEEDS

DOWN

From the hillside to the sea
Let your love wash over me
Over rivers, mountains high
Watch it drifting through the sky

Tide rolls out, tide rolls in
Let your love inside begin to grow
Let it bloom, into something beautiful

Baby baby just
Cool me, cool me, cool me down
Cool me down, cool me down

Let your love wash over me
wash over me

Feel your seasons changing me
Winter fires and autumn leaves
A sweet sunrise is what you bring
You shine your light for all to see

Tide rolls out, tide rolls in
Let your love inside begin to grow
Let it bloom, into something beautiful

Chorus

Lyrics by Barnaby Weir
Music by The Black Seeds

BUTTE

ARIZONA

SAL...

PHOENIX
64.3/38.2
103.5/77.5

ALBU...

OKLAHOMA CITY
47.2/28.3
93.1/71.8

LITTLE

LOU...

On the Road with...

Bic Runga

Get

From her
Where
Any wher
where
Stranded
Whistling

This side is for the

"Get some sleep" is
all about touring and being
on the road in the U.S. I was
living in New York and travelling to
gigs for a couple of years. Sometimes I
travelled by train, around the eastern sea board.
Places I recall off the top of my head were Boston,
Pennsylvania, Washington D.C. On the west coast I was in
L.A. San Diego, Portland, Seattle. I've played a lot
through Texas and the Mid West too. If I rattle my brain
I remember being in Albuquerque, New Mexico, Phoenix, Louisville
The whole thing is a blur now, I was barely awake
at the time! the song is about really sleep deprived.
have fun even though you're best really sleep deprived.

KATZ'S
DELICATESSEN
SINCE 1888

MAGIC CASTLE

HOTEL ✦ SUITES

HOME AGAIN - SHIHAD

PUT YOUR CLOCK BACK FOR THE WINTER
SHE ASKS WHEN I'LL BE HOME AGAIN
IF I COULD SEE THOSE EYES
I KNOW THEY'D CUT ME DOWN TO SIZE
YOU'RE NOT HERE WHEN I NEED YOU

SO SIT AND WAIT
AND BEND AND BREAK
AND RISE AND FALL
JUST YOU - THAT'S ALL
I'M HERE, YOU'RE THERE
DON'T MEAN I DON'T CARE
I'M SO SORRY. I WAS MILES AWAY

IT'S BEEN A DAY OF TINY TRIUMPHS
IT'S BEEN A WEEK SPENT IN DESPAIR
BUT YOU CAN'T SEND IT DOWN A PHONELINE
I DO MY BEST BUT I'M NOT THERE

SO SLEEP AND WAKE
AND DREAM UP YOUR FATE
AND RISE AND FALL
WATCH YOU GROW TALL
I'M HERE, YOU'RE THERE
BUT YOU SHOULD KNOW I STILL LOVE YOU
WHEN I'M MILES AWAY

I'LL BE HOME AGAIN.

HOLLYWOOD CA 90028

SHIHAD

We wrote the music to this tune while living
in LA at a place called the Magic Hotel.
We had our gear set up in a studio out in the
San Fernando Valley on a ghetto blaster we
took from the hotel, and this was one of the special ones that we all loved.
I remember being pretty homesick there (which is what the song's about) but
also, at the time, coming to realize the effect of the band being away all
the time was having on our partners back home.

When we got back to NZ it sat around on a cassette for ages
while the other guys waited for me to put some singing on it.
When it came time to record what became the "Fish" album, I left
it until the last minute in the studio to
write the lyrics which, luckily, all came
at once and "Home Again" was born.

x JON

This is us, recording the choruses of April Sun in 1977.

I remember going out into the recording room and taking this shot of Marc while he was singing the main vocal. Paul caught this bolt of lightning and wrangled it into a song with a divine structure, lyric and melody.

Now, over 30 years later, a totally different Dragon plays April Sun.

As every voice in the room belts out the chorus,

Marc and Paul live on in this song.

Todd Hunter

HELLO
my name is

APRIL SUN IN CUBA
P. HEWSON   M. HUNTER

I'm tired of the city life
Summer's on the run
People tell me I should stay
But I got to get my fun
So don't try to hold me back
There's nothing you can say
Snake eyes on the paradise
And we got to go today

Take me to the April sun in Cuba
Take me where the April sun
Gonna treat me
So right

I can almost smell the perfumed nights
And see the starry sky
I wish you coming with me baby
'Cause right before my eye
Castro in the alley way
Talkin' 'bout missile love
Talkin' 'bout JFK
And the way they shook him up
I'm tired of the city life
Summer's on the run
Birds in the winter sky
Are heading for the sun
Oh we can stick it out
In this cold + grey
Snake eyes on the paradise
And we got to go today
Take me to the April sun
C'mon take me
Take me to the April sun

DRAGON
APRIL SUN IN CUBA
(Hunter-Marc Hunter) April
Portrait LP "Running"

Portrait
AN AUSTRALIAN PERFORMANCE
Time: 3.24
PR 45008
© 1977
Australian Record
Company Limited
MX179379
45

BATHE
IN THE
RIVER

Like a bird
Through prison bars
I'm escaping
And behind me
on the long highway
Lies all that I've forsaken
Cool river, glow
I am bound for wherever you go

I'm gonna bathe in the river
Gonna hold my head up
in the river
Not gonna worry any more
Gonna reach that golden shore

I don't feel afraid
For now I see
That if I believe
I will be free
Wide river, glow
I'm gonna learn
whatever you know

Ch.

Mighty river
hear that rushin' sound
Cool clear water
lay my burden down

Ch.

Although perfectly
created for the
movie 'NO.2',
Bathe in the river
took on a life of
its own far beyond
this.
Don created a
powerful & Beautiful
Piece that is widely
relevant throughout our
different background &
cultures in New Zealand.
It became an anthem
with much meaning to
many people. I'm proud to
be a part of it.

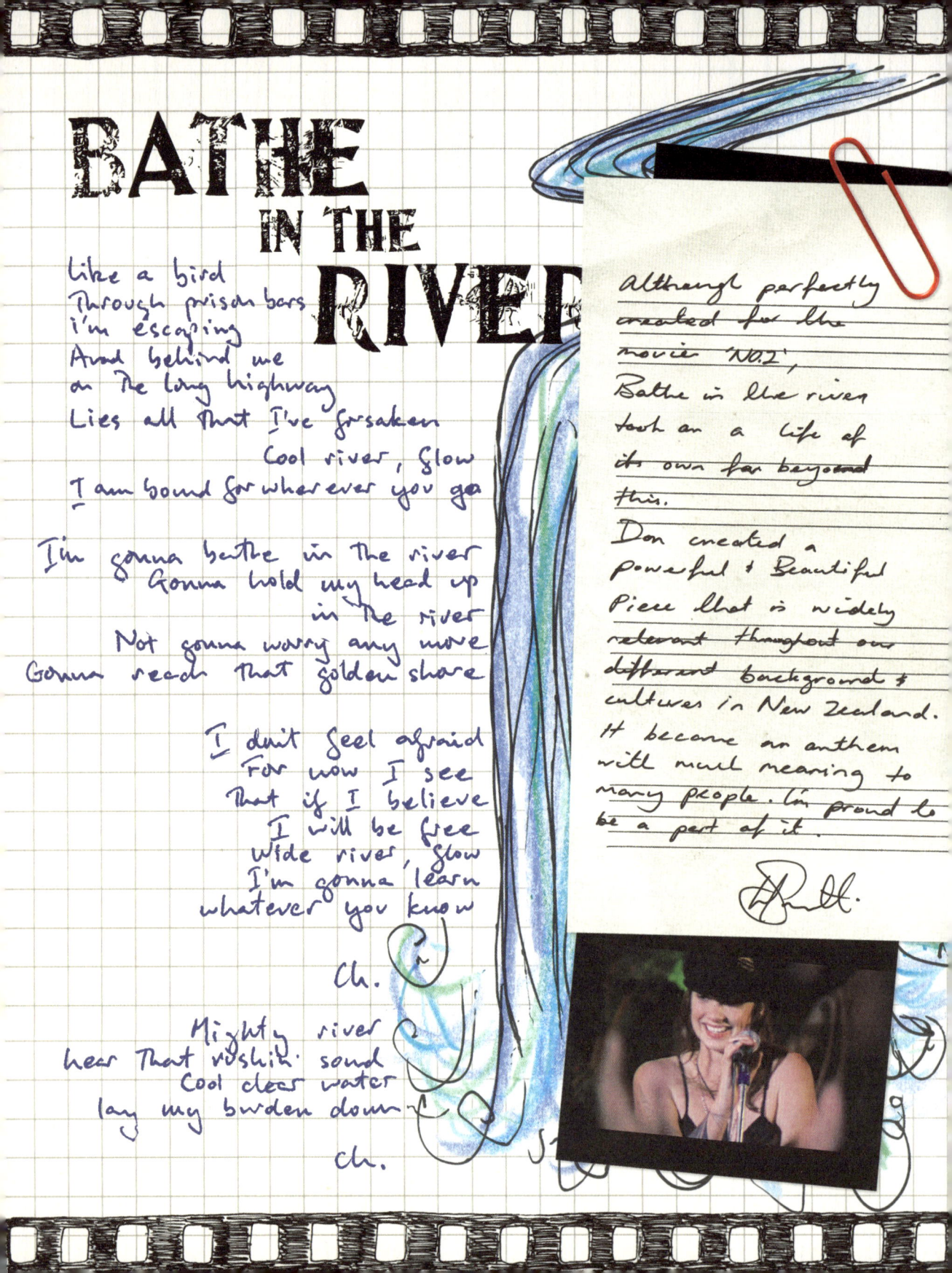

Toa Fraser wanted a song for his film "No.2". He thought he'd have to buy some big shiny overseas thing, but I said "I've always wanted to write a Gospel song — give me a few days." Bathe In The River is what came out. Rivers turn up in songs to mean lots of things: distance, longing, cleansing, baptism, even death. With this one I was trying to get all of that in there, plus the idea of a teeming rush of people, that the singer realises she's part of — and all she needs to do is step in with her head up to "the human world, really. Sort of a love song.

I wouldn't normally write anything that straight-up, but Toa's film gave me permission.

Later that year, when I was finishing the rest of the music for the film, Toa had the idea of asking Hollie Smith to do the vocal. She did a fantastic job, the film came out, and the song was a hit.

SONG	Bathe In The River
SONGWRITER	Don McGlashon
PERFORMERS	HOLLIE SMITH

with The Mount Raskill Preservation Society

(The Jubilation Choir, Bella Kalolo, Jason Smith SJD, Willy Scott, David Long, Toby Laing, Steve Roche, Stephen Small and Don McGlashon)

Since then, it's been sung by school choirs, translated into Te Reo for the National Kapa haka championships, and sung at the ceremony for the handing back of the Waikato River to Tainui.

DMcG.

PRESS

MARAC
● Financiers
● Merchant Bankers
● Expert / Import Finance

quod non honestum

THURSDAY, MARCH 29, 1979.

to

Spit Enz in

tour" aga

though the New
rock group, Sp
lost $11,000 of unin
d guitars and per-
tion equipment in a
at the time of the
bassa Music and Arts
ival in January, the
usiasm of the group is
paired.
Christchurch briefly
e setting out on a 10-
New Zealand tour
ting at Timaru today,
Enz is "running
according to a mem-
r of the band, Eddie
yner.
he group has just com-
d a 39-date Australian
of clubs and pubs
has released a new
called "Frenzy"
is selling well
the Tasman.
use of the loss of
ipment at Nam-
he group has had
instruments, ad-
the cost of the

Spe
min

r, the costumes
the band is
re not affected.
lic-address sys-
ts are in Brit-

ithout a s and
gnes, th late the
b Enz S 3 900.
s more than as a
a bail with out n
costume a it,
he "split."
An R e r
that tour
even ces
centres a Na
75 per c
"It wo as
for us as
to come out
Split En
only two shows
since last March b e
the band was getting
through business diffi-
culties. A difference of
opinion arose between the
group and the record com-
pany, Chrysalis, about
whether Split Enz should
do another album or re-
lease singles.
The band wanted to do
an album, and so Chry-
salis did not take up its
option to keep on the
band, said Eddie Rayner.
At present the band's
albums are being handled
by Mushroom Records in
Australia A progressive
record has grown an

Nigel Griggs

Tim Finn

THE

ZEALAND

Nihil utile

Petrol expected t
rise 6c a litre
within six week

...price of petrol will rise about 6c a litre with
...ex...x weeks as a result of the increases ann...
...on...day by the Organisation of Petroleum Ex...

...Mr Birch...pact of the oil crisis on top of th...
...on New Zealand would be-...increase.
...less and less until it But Sau...
...levelled out with the rest world's big...
...sical music as well as ...er, said it...
...and rock...floor pr...
...the tribunal. Active bosses say they Welfare...
If it is piped into all student have taken note.

Split Enz rouses fervou

Split Enz delivers again

revie...

Zealand...t Enz...recorded the added extra...
the count...s the t Enz one of New Zea...
...rch with...songs successful bands.
...ferent act...His quiet humour showe...
expertise in an excellent duo...
...ew album...voice from stage with keyboards man Eddie...
...February with...o...y in front holding the stage with fingers...
...tour behin...round et...The audience, after a long wait...
..."Frenzy" with the headlining band to appear,...
...eir first..me as the better know Split Enz a reception bordering
...5 months and...arlie," or the hard-hitting hysteria.
...months, Spli...us Brass." Cheers went up with every...
...0 people at the s...he easy, at-home manner of the whether known or unknown and...
...t it has not lost its edg...newest members of the group. En-...enthusiasm saw Split Enz play...
...plagued by equipment glishman Malcolm Green on drums and experimental arrangements of so...
...ter loosing all their instru-...bassist Nigel Griggs was a direct played close to pattern hundreds...
...fire at Waihi this week, the...contrast to the fast and furious pace as times before...
...rance on stage in brilliant...the youngest member, guitarist Neil And whatever people were look...
...costumes was one of impact.... Finn, raged up and down in real for, new developments or pure p...
...ched into the title track of..."Stranger Than Fiction" style. sure, Split Enz made sure they got i...
...um with antics that made it...His brother Tim, on vocals, caught K. P.
...which was moving quicker...crowd with a voice that showed his
...t or their fingers — and...pleasure to be home, especially a
...rough music from previ-...charismatic new song called Betty.
...with a style that gave yo...As usual, percussionist Noel Crombie

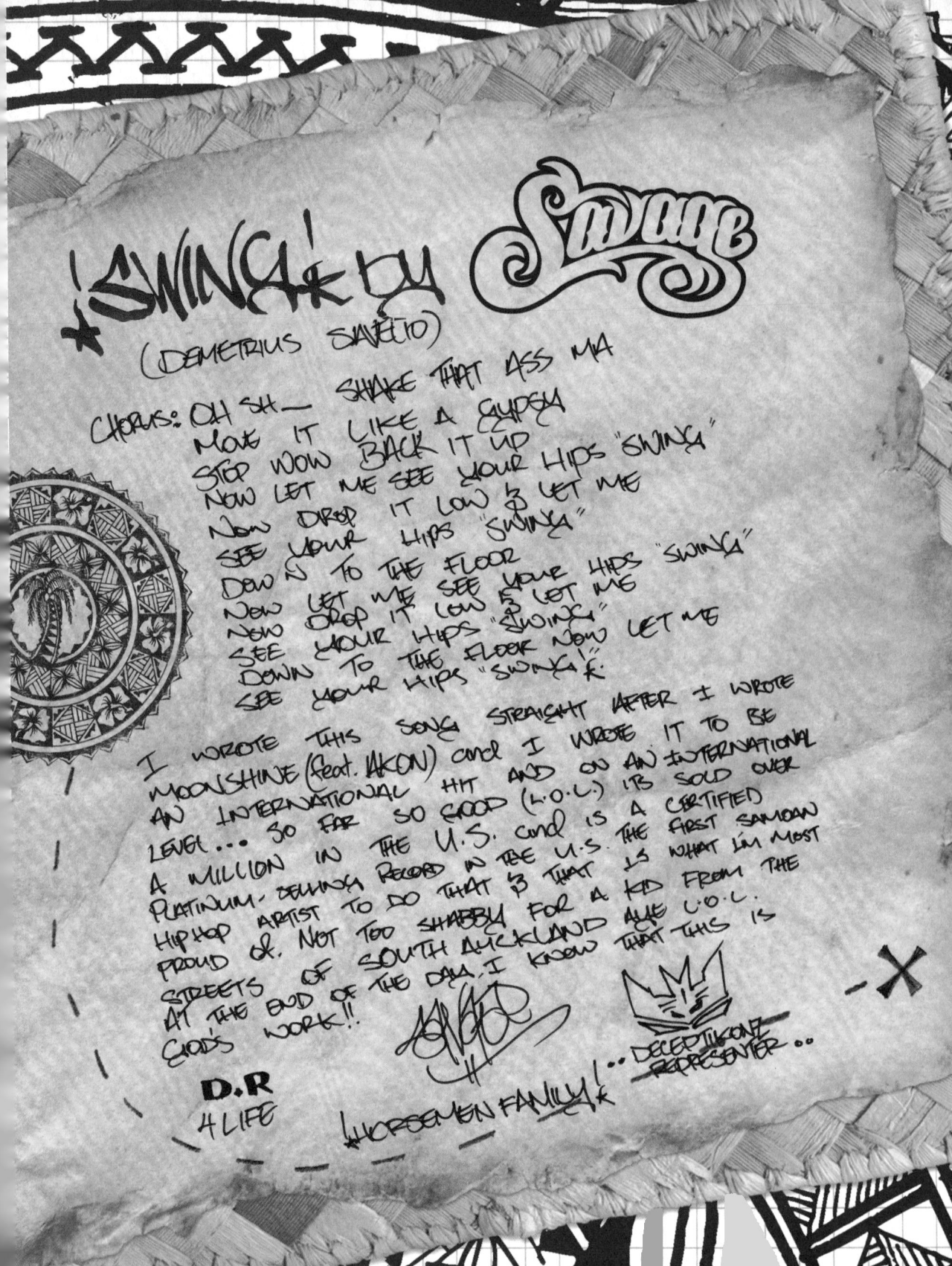

"SWING!" by Savage

(DEMETRIUS SAVELIO)

CHORUS: OH SH__ SHAKE THAT ASS MA
MOVE IT LIKE A GYPSY
STOP WOW BACK IT UP
NOW LET ME SEE YOUR HIPS "SWING"
NOW DROP IT LOW & LET ME
SEE YOUR HIPS "SWING"
DOWN TO THE FLOOR
NOW LET ME SEE YOUR HIPS "SWING"
NOW DROP IT LOW & LET ME
SEE YOUR HIPS "SWING"
DOWN TO THE FLOOR NOW LET ME
SEE YOUR HIPS "SWING!".

I WROTE THIS SONG STRAIGHT AFTER I WROTE
MOONSHINE (feat. AKON) and I WROTE IT TO BE
AN INTERNATIONAL HIT AND ON AN INTERNATIONAL
LEVEL... SO FAR SO GOOD (L.O.L.) ITS SOLD OVER
A MILLION IN THE U.S. and IS A CERTIFIED
PLATINUM-SELLING RECORD IN THE U.S. THE FIRST SAMOAN
HIP HOP ARTIST TO DO THAT & THAT IS WHAT I'M MOST
PROUD OF. NOT TOO SHABBY FOR A KID FROM THE
STREETS OF SOUTH AUCKLAND AYE L.O.L.
AT THE END OF THE DAY I KNOW THAT THIS IS
GOD'S WORK!!

D.R
4 LIFE

#HORSEMEN FAMILY #

..DECEPTIKONZ
REPRESENT..

-X

Venus G G $^{(F\#)}$ F C

Come my little venus
Can't you feel it's in all of us
like the light we'll see you soon
give up yourself and dive into the moon

and I don't mind
being with you
knowing I'm
by myself
there's a river
in all of us
that's dry,
as you are in me.

Come my little venus
wrapped in shadows
  Now you're one of us
I hear the footsteps inside your head
walking trying to find yourself
  I found myself in you
    let me in, let me breathe
I found myself in you.

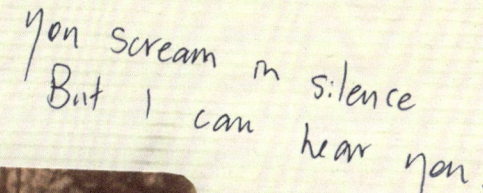

You scream in silence
But I can hear you.

James
+x

TALLER THAN GOD STRAWPEOPLE AS I WAS DRIVING TO YO
PLACES UNKNOWN ACCELERATING THOUGHTS OF YOU REM
TO YOUR HOME I DON'T BELIEVE THAT HEAVEN WAITS ABOVE
YOU DISGUISE WITH SHEETS FOR CURTAINS BOOKS ALL S
THAT WAY CAUSE YOU'RE **TALLER THAN GOD** COUNTING THE
WAIT ANY MORE TASTE YOUR SHADOW FEEL YOU MOVE
COUNTING THE STEPS THAT LEAD TO YOUR DOOR I DON
BELIEVE BUT MAYBE IT'S THE ROOM THAT YOU DISGUI
ALL STACKED AWAY YOU'RE MY SAVIOUR WHEN YOU LOOK
TALLER THAN GOD AS I WAS DRIVING MY WAY TO YOUR

MUSIC AND LYRICS BY PAUL CASSERLY AND FIONA M

this was a song Fiona Mcdonald wrote that
we reworked for the Vicarious album.
Victoria Kelly added the beautiful string arrangement.
You can see the video that Justin Pemberton made
for it on YouTube. Fiona plays a motel owner
and I'm some sort of dodgy doctor.

Pau

HOME WE'RE IN A RIVER OF PEOPLE AND CARS DRIVING TO
BERED SKIN BREATHING FUMES AS I WAS DRIVING MY WAY
THE SKY I DON'T BELIEVE BUT MAYBE IT'S IN A ROOM THAT
CKED AWAY YOU'RE MY SAVIOUR WHEN YOU LOOK AT ME
STEPS THAT LEAD TO YOUR DOOR SEVENTEEN DAYS CAN'T
BREATHE YOUR NAME CAUSE YOU HUNG THE MOON
BELIEVE THAT HEAVEN WAITS ABOVE THE SKY I DON'T
WITH SHEETS FOR   CURTAINS BOOKS
AT ME THAT WAY   CAUSE YOU'RE
HOME

DONALD

Strawpeople
Taller Than God

XPR 3154
XPR 3154A
31-003154-20
45 RPM

epic
© 0199

A1 | Vocal Club Mix
A2 | Instrumental

6:20
6:20

I: SO BITTER-SWEET
LOST FOR THE MINUTE

UNNATURALLY WEAK
GIVE IN TO YOUR SMILE
I WANT TO DISCOVER
WHAT WE MEAN TO EACH OTHER
PLEASE LET ME LOVE
        LOVE
    FOR A WHILE

II: WE'RE 2 OF A KIND

FOR A WHILE

WRITTEN BY BOH RUNGA
FOR stellar*

BUT SOMETHING LIKE STRANGERS
MISFIT AND BLIND
STILL FINDING OUR FEET
WE DON'T KNOW THE LIMIT
COS WE'RE BOTH LIVING IN IT
PLEASE LET ME LOVE
        LOVE
    FOR A WHILE

I CAN'T HELP, CAN'T HELP MYSELF WHEN
        I'M W/ YOU,
DON'T YOU KNOW, I CAN'T LET YOU GO
YOU'RE ONE MISTAKE I'M ALWAYS MAKING
YOU GOT IN ME ALL YOU NEED
ALL YOU EVER NEED

I had this great idea for a song, just a couple of verses really, and a pretty melody. I took it to the guys in stellar* and played it to them. They liked it. "Finish it, Boh, it's good." "OK." But I didn't. I lost my capo. And forgot about it.

"What happened to that **FOR A WHILE** tune you played us?"

"Oh, oh I lost my capo. I gotta buy another one. Yeah, yeah, I'll finish it. Yep, sweet as." But I didn't. Forgot about it.

"Have you finished that song?"

"Oh man, well, no. No, not yet. I will, tho!"

Anyway, **A WHILE** went by and a frustrated Andrew Maclaren* turned up at m♥y door with a little paper bag.

FOR A WHILE

"Finish that song. I bought you a bloody capo." When it came time to record it, I got another idea....

Bring ~ ring ~ brr...ring RING

"'Ello?"

"Hey, is this Andy Lovegrove? (from BREAKS Co-OP)" RING

"Yeah..."

"Hey, Andy, Boh Runga here."

"Aw, hey Boh, how are you, mate?"

"Good thank you. Look, I was wondering, would you consider singing a duet w/ me? A song for the new stellar* record?"

"Really? Well, yeah, sure mate, okay...."

"Great! I'll come get you!"

* drummer from stellar*

Counting The Beat

THE

LOOK AT ˇSUNRISE , LOOK AT IT BURN
I LOOK INTO YOUR EYES, DON'T KNOW WHERE TO TURN
I'M GONNA DRIFT INTO THAT VOID
I'M FLYIN' THROUGH SPACE, I'M AN ASTEROID
I'M THINKING ABOUT YOU AND NOTHING ELSE
THINKING ABOUT YOU, YOU'RE THINKIN' 'BOUT ME
THINKING ABOUT YOU, I'M COUNTING THE BEAT
THINKING 'BOUT YOU THINKIN' 'BOUT ME
THINKIN' 'BOUT JUST YOU & ME, LA DA DE DE
THERE AIN'T NO PLACE I'D RATHER BE

LA DA DEDA — ETC

I'M BLEEDING TO DEATH, ON A CLOUDLESS DAY
A THREE/FOUR HEARTBEAT, A WALTZIN' AWAY
OOHH OH —ETC
I'M COUNTING THE BEAT 2, 3, 4, 5
I'M FEELIN' THE HEAT, GLAD TO BE ALIVE
I'M COUNTING THE BEAT, I'M WISHING THAT YOU
THAT YOU WERE MINE
THINKING ABOUT YOU ＞ ETC
JUST YOU & ME, LA DA DE DE
THERE AIN'T NO PLACE I'D RATHER BE
LA DA DE DA X INFINITUM

THE SWINGERS

....jamming at a soundcheck
in Palmerston Nth circa 1979...
a dumb rockabilly riff. Others present
spontaneously start dancing around...
a signal that this ditty is
POPular. I throw some chords at Bones'
bass pattern. All pretty much done
in 10 minutes flat. At the time
I'm reading a book by English poet
Robert Graves.That night after the gig
I read a poem entitled
'Counting The Beats'...I steal
the title,cloudless day &
bleeding to death !!
Some songs write themselves others
are a labour of love...
this is the former. The Swingers end up
in severe debt 2 years later. Only 15 years
later when K-mart use it as ad-music
do we make a buck out of it. !!

It was a wonderful session at
E.M.I. in late 1969 recording this song.
We wanted an acoustic organic type
of sound. The Studio was full of
cardboard boxes, shoes, matchboxes,
quaint little organs. (That was us!!)
lots of acoustic guitars, auto harp.
and Peter Dawking, producer.

The song is in Ab minor because
my nylon string guitar had been run
over and bent so it could only
be tuned a semitone flat without
it turning into a Jacque Tati boat!!.
1. 2. 3. all play together. Overdub
the shoe (hi-hat), matchbox (snare)
auto harp, swishy cymbals, Carl and
me singing in unison, and hey presto —
a real recording.

Wayne 2008.

Wayne

Through falling leaves I pick my way

V1   slowly

Talking aloud eases my mind

Sunlight filters through I feel my heart

                    is bursting

So full of thoughts I've thought

What am I going to do, I need some thoughts

                    that are new

do do do do do do do do do do do

do do do do do do

Ch. dee dee dee dee dee dee dee dee dee

dee de Nature enter me

Up in a tree a bird sings so sweetly

Nature's own voice I hear

V2 Rustling whistling leaves turning breeze to

talk to me now ease my mind.   speed

what am I going to do

I need some thoughts that are new.

Chorus

NOT
MANY

SCRIBE

"How many dudes you know roll like this?

..Not many.. If Any!"

Originally this song was just an intro to "The Crusader" however its popularity grew so fast we decided to make the remix. Featuring Savage & Con-Psy.
7 days ~~from~~ 'The Remix' concept
after

We had recorded the song & finished the video.
The original version of this track was inspired by my love for Christchurch city & the Canterbury, region.

x   Malo Lufutu

damn the river its wild ways
took my love & it ran away
I followed through this thought for days
... never found a thing

but you... you will find me here
resting my head, & sleeping
in a river bed

damn the river I'm giving up
'cause I've had it up to here will all this noise
& all you fucking boys playing with your toys
get so loud, I just gotta leave the room

and you.....; you will find me here
resting my head 😮 &
sleeping in a ⟨ river bed. {etc etc etc}

the static clatter
of the anti-matter
the pitter patter of your mind
I lie awake, trying to take
it all in.

IT'S ABOUT TWO MINUTES BRO.....

GUTTER BLACK - THE TRUE STORY

'PONSONBY REGGAE'... LIFE AS WE KNEW IT IN POST-COLONIAL BRITISH WEST PONSONBY; ROUGH, DISLOCATED, AND FRAUGHT WITH THE TENSION AND HUMIDITY OF A CRICKET PITCH IN KINGSTON.

I WAS 21 YEARS OLD. THE SONG WAS THEN 'SICKNESS BENEFIT' – WELL, OK, A SATIRE WITH BENEFIT ABUSE AS ITS CORE SUBJECT. HALF THE OLD VILLAS IN PONSONBY WERE FILLED WITH TEENAGE DROP-OUTS, DOPE FIENDS, PAINTERS, POETS, ADDICTS, WILD GAYS, TRANNIES AND ALCOHOLICS, AND THE OTHER HALF WORKED TO SUPPORT THEM. WE DIDN'T MIND. GRAHAM WAS A DUSTMAN; I DROVE A TRACTOR AT WESTERN SPRINGS, BUT GOT SACKED FOR STONED DRIVING AND SWIPING TOO MANY TREES. AT LEAST WE GOT TO SEE THE STONES FOR FREE, WHILE MY OLD MAN PUT UP ALL THE MONEY TO PROMOTE THE SHOW, AS THE BANKER FOR THE LATE IMPRESARIO, PHIL WARREN.

RESCUED FROM OUR ENDLESS PARTY-HALL CIRCUIT AND FREQUENT TRIPS TO PLAY IN CHRISTCHURCH, WHICH WE ABSOLUTELY LOVED, A KIND-HEARTED RECORD PRODUCER FROM ENGLAND GOT OUR LITTLE PAEAN TO THE HOMELESS, THE SICK, AND THE DISORIENTATED, AND GAVE IT A RADICAL NEW DIRECTION, A POP SONG WITH A LOVE THEME, HOWEVER ODDLY AMBIGUOUS.

IT WAS UNAVOIDABLE THAT I WAS TO IMBUE THE LYRICAL CONTENT WITH MY SPIRITUAL LEANINGS AT THE TIME. I WAS A LAPSED BUDDHIST – UNABLE TO RISE ABOVE THE PIT OF SENSE-GRATIFICATION AND THE TEMPORARY DUALITY OF BEING, YOU IN MY BRAIN, YOU IN MY HEART! MY LUCK IN THE GUTTER, BLACK, FREEMAN BAY (SIC) PIDGIN FOR NO HOPE AT ALL, I GUESS I'M RUNNING BACK TO YOU, DOWN THE GUTTER, TO THE RIVER, TO THE MIGHTY OCEAN, GOD AND BLISS, OR DEATH. THAT IS LIFE, THE SECOND WE'RE BORN, WE ARE IN THE WHIRL; SAMSARA, THE BUDDHISTS CALL IT. WE BEGIN THE PROCESS OF CHANGE, THROUGH TIME AND AGE, IN THE FLESH, DOWN THE RIVER OF LIFE, TO BE FINALLY RELEASED BACK INTO THE OCEAN OF BLISS. THAT IS THE SIGNIFICANCE OF THE GANGES, THE GODDESS, THE MOTHER, CARRYING HER CHILDREN HOME. AND, TO WIT! ALL SAILORS ARE BURIED AT SEA.

IN AUGUST 1976 MY DEAR BROTHER PHILIP WAS TRAGICALLY KILLED IN A CAR ACCIDENT IN SYDNEY, JUST DAYS BEFORE HELLO SAILOR'S FIRST ALBUM PRESSING, SO I WAS ABLE TO DEDICATE GUTTER BLACK TO HIM. HE HAD GONE TO SEA – RUNNING BACK, JUST AS THE TIDE HAD DELIVERED HIM INTO MY MOTHER'S WOMB. THAT IS THE BEAUTY OF LIFE, AND IT IS TRULY REMARKABLE THAT THE PUNTERS SING ALONG WITH THE MISTAKEN SUBSTITUTION OF LOVE FOR LUCK, "MY LOVE IN THE GUTTER BLACK." BUT THAT'S OK, I AM DELIRIOUSLY HAPPY FOR THE INSPIRATION FROM THE SEA, AND FREEMANS BAY, AND FROM WHOMEVER I WAS LOVING AT THE TIME.

Gutter Black

— Dave McArtney

Lyin' in the gutter
I cut the cord from my mother
She pat me on de head and said,
"Go to sea boy, get to sea, man"

Barbra O'Reilly
She come into my house,
Trouble, trouble, trouble!
Go to sea boy, get to sea, man

My Luck in the gutter, black
I guess I'm runnin' back
To you
You in my Brain
You in my Heart!

Long Windjammers
Sailing on de ocean
Cool breeze blowin' yeah
Go to sea Man, some don't come back
My Luck in the gutter, black
I guess I'm runnin' back
To You
You in my brain
You in my Heart!

EVERMORE
"It's too Late"

this song reminds me of Feilding every
now and then. The sweeping calm isolation
somehow came thru on the recording.
It was written in a east-facing
sun room on a beaten old Tama 6-string.
Circa... November 2003... I think.

Dann Hume

Am   Em
Monday morning, hesitate
    Dm   Am
I can't get out of bed
   Am   Em
I'd rather go back to the dreams
      Dm   Am
I'm living in my head — yeah

Tuesday evening, pack my bags
I'm heading out the door
I left a box of memories
Lying on the floor — yeah

Am Em   Dm   Am
Ride on,   ride til early morning sun
    Am Em   Bm   Am
Ride on, like the dawning of the day
    Bm C   F   Am   C
It's too late to let all your feelings show
   Am Em   Dm   Am
Go on, 'til the night is swept away

I'm running from the city lights
  I'm running from this empty life
  I'm running out of time tonight
  I'm screaming out for "HELP! HELP!"

["Slow down you're moving too fast,
    Go home, you'll feel better for it
  Oh boy, you better stop dreaming
    It's all in your head!"

                F
Cos it's too late now...   CHORUS

Ride On, run til early morning sun
  Ride on, like the morning of the day
  It's too late to let all your feelings show
  Ride on til the night is swept away

CHORDS:
12-string tuned half step down
    to D#

Stones like these are just like hell underground

There's a story
I know, We all leave
And let go, there is
Nothing to hold us
In a Moment of time
When the fruit becomes
Wine and the thought
Become the memory

my love you will be still Demon in my ear you will be too

Moon you are half you will be hell Ghost of

GOLDENHORSE

Maybe Tomorrow

All of your sorrow
Maybe Tomorrow will fade
Away in the air, Trying to please
Me, Making it easy, It won't
Be there It won't be there
In your life!

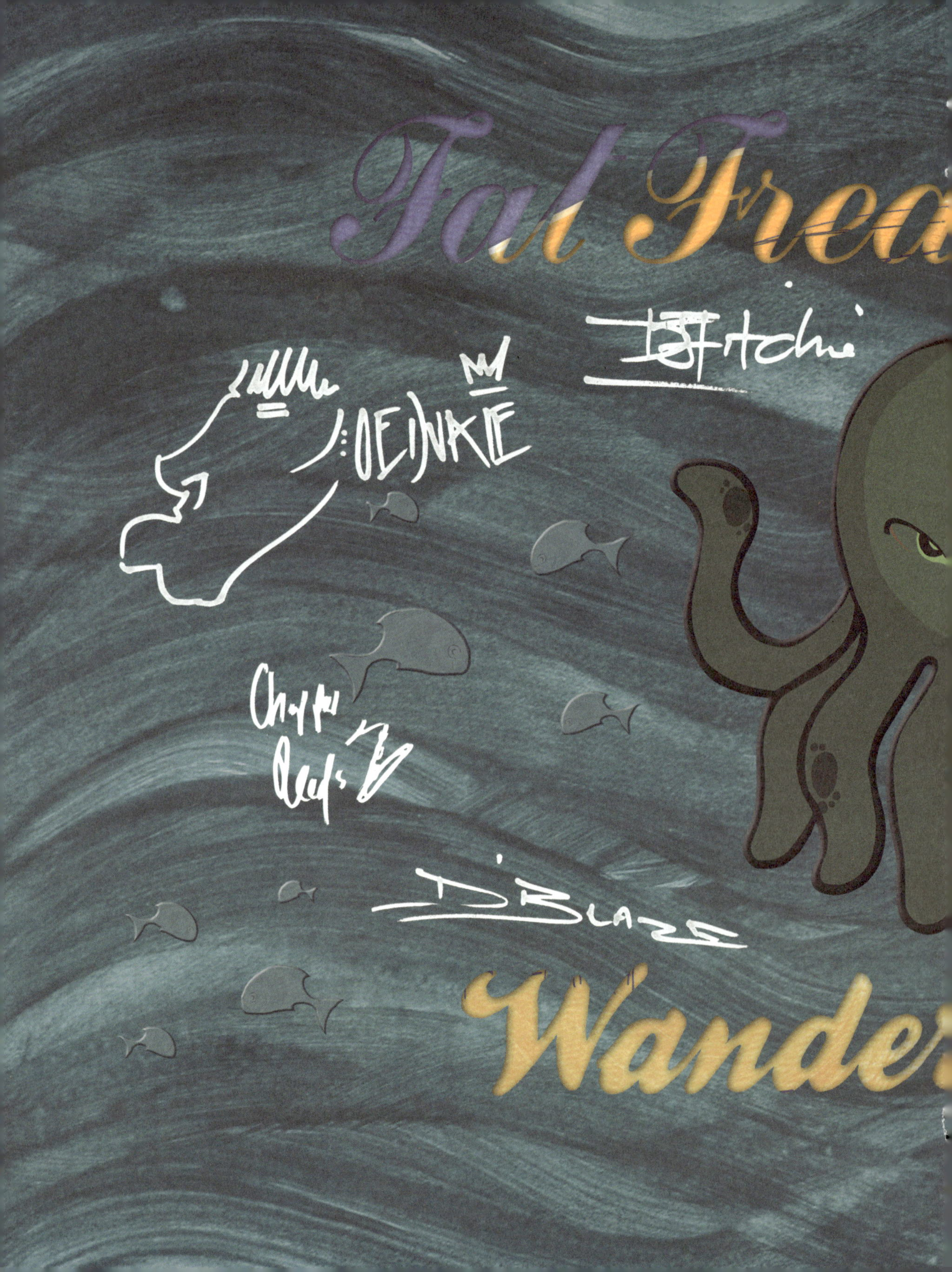
Fat

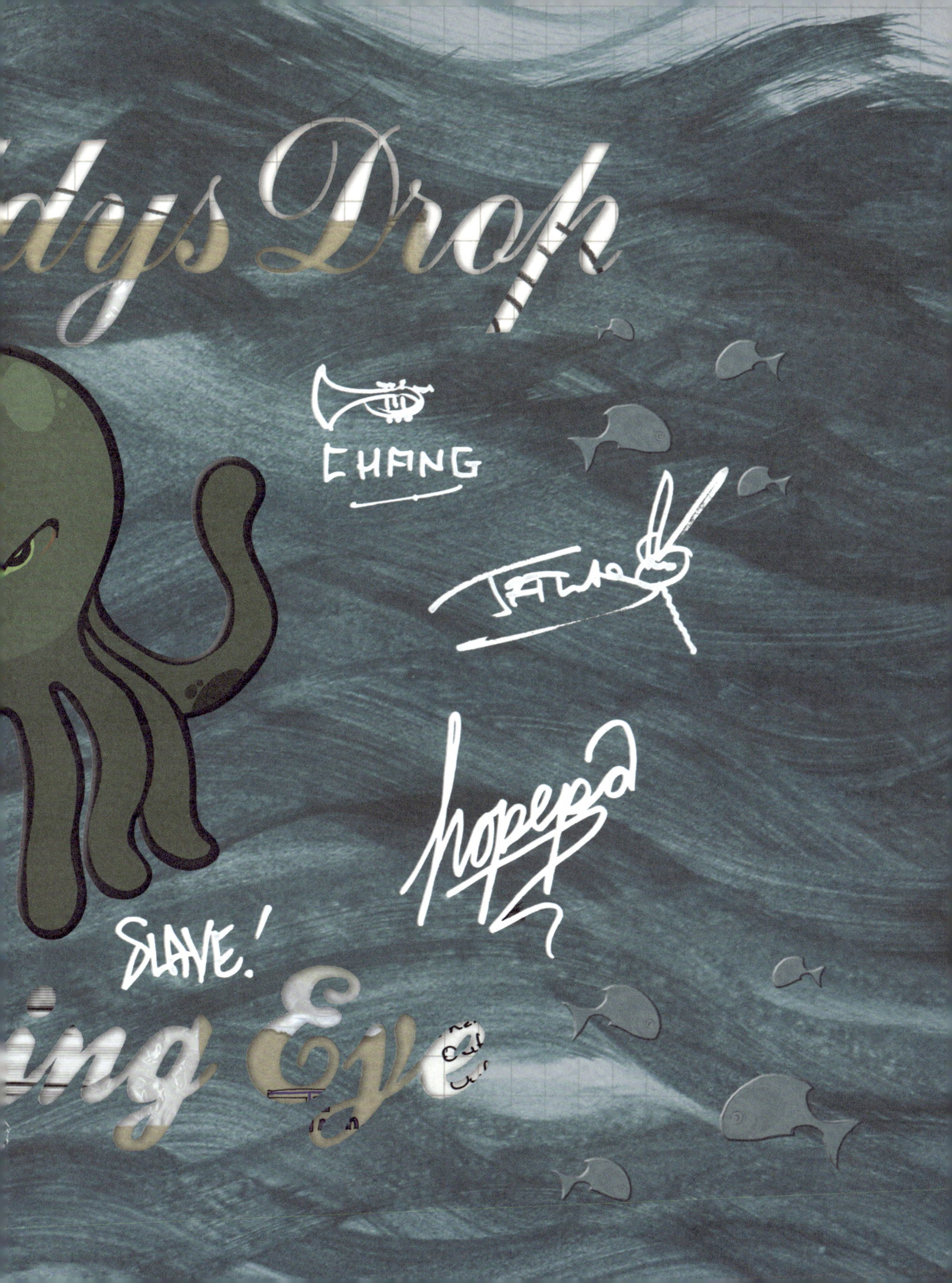
dys Drop
CHANG
SLAVE!
ing Eye

Out Of This W

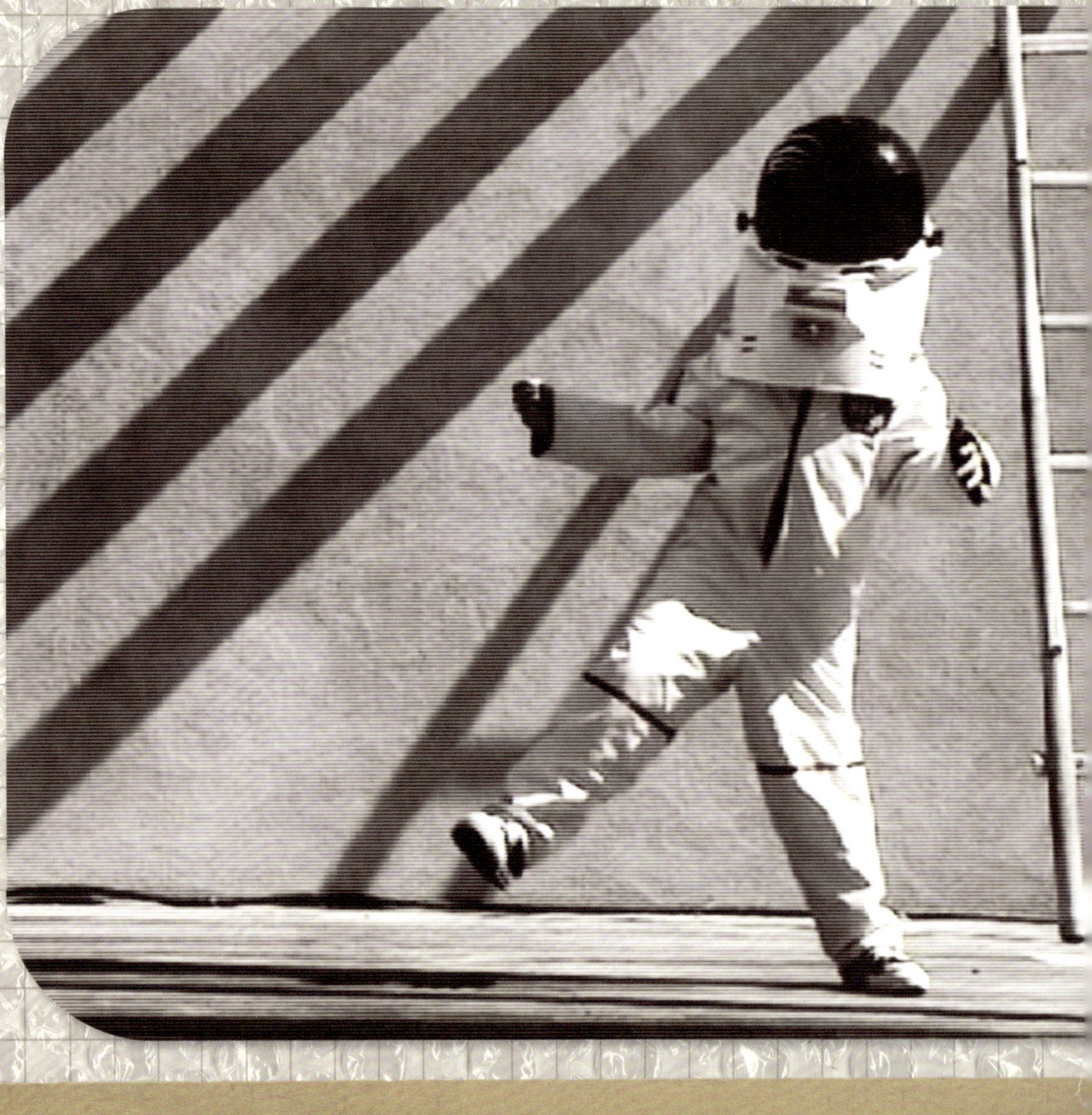

orld

There's vapour flowing like a bridal gown
From the rocket-ship that we're counting down
And love is leaving for the cold of space
It's a mystery, it's our saving grace

Out of this World with you
Searching for life I never knew

Out of this world it's true
There's no limit on the things we'll do

Out of this world
It's only when I look into your eyes
I can see beyond what I fear inside
And I love the way that you reminded me

How it all belongs to eternity
Out of this world with you

Searching for life we never knew
Out of this world it's true

There's no limit on the things we'll do
Out of this World
Out of this World
Out of this World with you (T. Finn)

Finn.

Hey I got a lot of faith in you
I'll stick with you kid - that's the bottom line
Yeah you have a lot of fun don't you?
And living with you is a ball of a time

Hey beauty when the mood gets you down
Your bottom lip's near dragging on the ground
That's when I've gotta play the clown for you
Black humour made you kick your blues
Howdy angel - where did you hide your wings

Her (love) shines over my horizon
she's a slice of 'heaven'?
Warm moonlight over my horizon
she's a slice of heaven

Dave
Slice

Her "love" shine
she's a slice
warm moonligh
she's a slice

FooTroT
FlaTs ™
The Dog's Tail Tale

Dobbyn
Heaven

Hey I got a lot of faith in you
I'll stick with you kid – that's the bottom line
Yeah we have a lot of (fun) doin' it we
And heaven has to be with you all the time
Hey beauty when the mood gets your down
Your bottom lip's near dragging on the ground
That's when I gotta play the clown for you
[Black] humour made me kick my blues
Howdy angel – where did you hide your wings

ver my horizon
eaven
ver my horizon
eaven

I was writing the music for 'Footrot Flats' and this one wouldn't let me sleep.²²²²
I spent a lot of time working on the music bed in my studio at home in Sydney.
It seemed so right to invite the Herbs to sing on this one for the harmony.
'Graceland' was out that year so it had a small influence on the 'DaDaDa's'
I remember working at Wellington's Marmalade Studios with Bruce Lynch
and being filmed whilst recording. There were two other film crews there
also and having make-up applied when mixing a record is a little strange.
I had a great belief it would be a radio hit – what clinched it was the
movie trailer – people insisted that radio play it and it was somewhat
ironic that a major station at the time wouldn't play it, even though it was
top of their own chart. They finally rolled and the rest is history. The
Ozzies loved it too. So in many ways it was a hit in the traditional sense.
That is – it was hypeless. People just wanted to hear it.
It sounds great live and I'm very proud of the lyric – especially DaDaDa.
Dave Dobbyn

HOME
Annah Mac

Its gonna be okay this time
Iim coming Home
Sick of all those city lights
Sleeping in a cold bed by the phone
I've been travelling through a long black tunnel
Re-emerging into the light
Won't believe that everyone will fall for me
In my glass slippers curfew set for midnight
Midnight

It's gonna be alright this time
Iim coming Home
Evoked among familiar faces
The sound of a Trombone
And in the presence of the night
I stove my feelings on the shelf
Listen to the breathing of the fireplace
No longer in a cold bed by myself

Iim Home
Home
Iim Home
And you can count
the seconds in my time
But Iim Home
Home and Iill be fine
Gotta get myself
Home

There's nothing else that I need
Just the warm familiar faces standing next to me
There's nowhere else Iid rather be
In the warmth & company
Of friends & family

Home
Home
Iim Home
And you can count the seconds in my time
But Iim home
Home & Iill be fine
Gotta get myself home

Quick question:

Factorise

1. $3x - 9y = 3(x - 3y)$ ✓
2. $4y^2 - y = y(4y - 1)$ ✓
3. $x^2 y - 3xy^2 = xy(x - 3y)$ ✓
4. $(x+y)^2 - 7(x+y) = (x+y)(1x+y - 7)$
5. $ab + ac = ba + bc$ $a(b+c) - b(d+c)$
6. $x^2 + 5x + 6$
7. $x^2 - 10x + 21$
8. $x^2 + 10x + 24$
9. $x^2 + 2x - 99$
10. $x^2 - x - 30$
11. 3 0% ☺ haha

$8x^2 + 10x = 3$
$-3 \qquad -3$
$8x^2 + 10x - 3 = 0$

$(2x + 3)(4x - 1) = 0$

either $2x + 3 = 0$
$2x = -3$
$x = \frac{-3}{2}$

or $4x$
4
x

My most productive songwriting times are always during **MATHS**

Home was written for Jessie Wakelin & the girls at Tolcarne boarding residence when I was 14 & in 3rd form, my first year away from home in Dunedin. Jessie asked me to make a song about going ame for holidays. I did.

Pokarekare Ana

Margaret Uslich

Pōkarekare ana
ngā wai o Waiapu,
Whiti atu koe hine
marino ana e.

E hine e
hoki mai ra
Ka mate ahau
I te aroha e.

Tuhituhi taku reta
tuku atu taku ringi
Kia kite tō iwi
raru raru ana e.

The bone carving my father made
me, a couple of years before he
died in 1996

I was taught t
I was te smal
1926 at Ahipara
Ana' originated

centre in New Lynn, West Auckland. We sang it in
strumming along on his guitar. We ended up winning
heaps of groceries. which for a family of nine or

'Pokarekare Ana' is a heartfelt song with a gorgeou
over the world. It is a song we can all be proud of

...ing 'Pokarekare Ana' by my father Victor, when [a] child. Dad, from the Nga Puhi tribe, was born in ...in Northland, not far from where 'Pokarekare ...from in 1914. For me, as one of seven children, music was always a big part of our family life and we kids were encouraged to sing for our relatives whenever they visited. Dad would always accompany us on either his acoustic guitar or our old upright piano.

Dad at about 30 yrs

My first public performance of 'Pokarekare Ana' was with my big brothers, Pat and Martin, when I was seven years old. It was at the annual talent quest at our local shopping ...three-part harmony, with Dad on stage with us, ...the competition. First prize was ten dollars, plus ...ight budget was greatly appreciated.

...elody. It is sung on stages and at gatherings an...

I wrote Better Be Home Soon one morning straight out of
about 30 minutes - always a good sign and a rare event
to lend itself well to a number of uses, a sense of longing
relationship break-ups bereavement but originally I was th...
a woman's perspective about someone who is just about ove...
husband . . . . mmm!

ed in
t seems
omesickness
ing from
n absentee

CROWDED HOUSE

Better Be Home Soon by Neil Finn

somewhere deep inside
something's got a hold of you
and it's pushing me aside
see it stretch on forever

I know I'm right
for the first time in my life
that's why I tell you
you'd better be home soon
stripping back the coats
of lies and deception
back to nothingness
like a week in the desert
I know I'm right
for the first time in my life
that's why I tell you
you'd better be home soon
don't say no, don't say nothing's wrong
when you get back home, maybe I'll be
                                    gone

It would cause me pain
if we were to end it
but I could start again
you can depend on it
I know I'm right
for the first time in my life
that's why I tell you
you'd better be home soon

LAST CENTURY

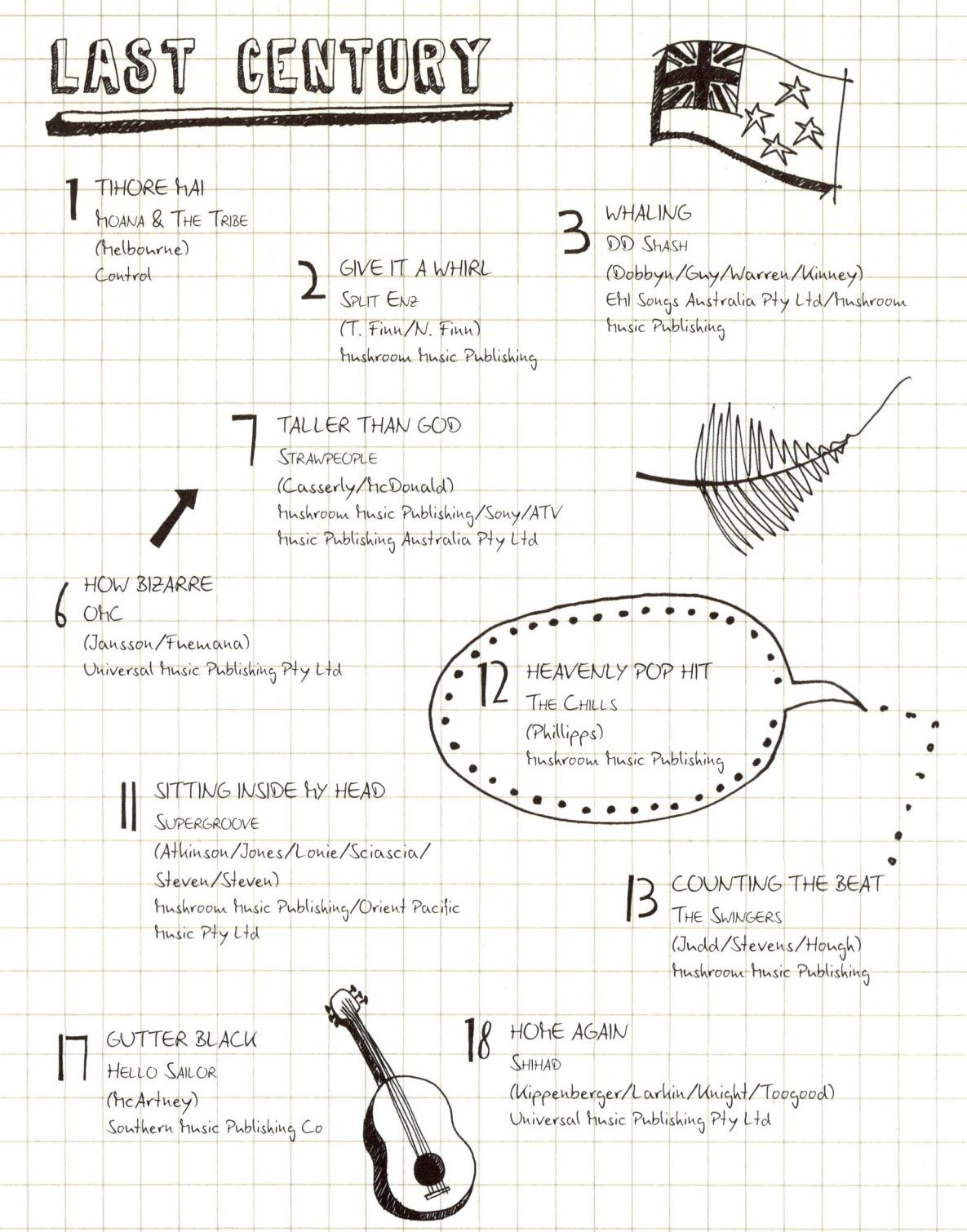

1 TIHORE MAI
MOANA & THE TRIBE
(Melbourne)
Control

2 GIVE IT A WHIRL
SPLIT ENZ
(T. Finn/N. Finn)
Mushroom Music Publishing

3 WHALING
DD SMASH
(Dobbyn/Guy/Warren/Kinney)
EMI Songs Australia Pty Ltd/Mushroom
Music Publishing

7 TALLER THAN GOD
STRAWPEOPLE
(Casserly/McDonald)
Mushroom Music Publishing/Sony/ATV
Music Publishing Australia Pty Ltd

6 HOW BIZARRE
OMC
(Jansson/Fuemana)
Universal Music Publishing Pty Ltd

12 HEAVENLY POP HIT
THE CHILLS
(Phillipps)
Mushroom Music Publishing

11 SITTING INSIDE MY HEAD
SUPERGROOVE
(Atkinson/Jones/Lonie/Sciascia/
Steven/Steven)
Mushroom Music Publishing/Orient Pacific
Music Pty Ltd

13 COUNTING THE BEAT
THE SWINGERS
(Judd/Stevens/Hough)
Mushroom Music Publishing

17 GUTTER BLACK
HELLO SAILOR
(McArtney)
Southern Music Publishing Co

18 HOME AGAIN
SHIHAD
(Kippenberger/Larkin/Knight/Toogood)
Universal Music Publishing Pty Ltd

4 DOMINION RD
THE MUTTONBIRDS
(McGlashan)
Native Tongue Music Publishing

5 WHY DOES LOVE DO THIS TO ME?
THE EXPONENTS
(Luck)
Sony/ATV Music Publishing Australia Pty Ltd

8 APRIL SUN IN CUBA
DRAGON
(Hunter/Hewson)
EMI Songs Australia Pty Ltd/Essex Music
Australia Pty Ltd

10 BREAK IN THE WEATHER
JENNY MORRIS
(J. Morris/T. Morris)
Universal Music Publishing Pty Ltd

9 SINNER
NEIL FINN
(Finn/De Vries)
Mushroom Music Publishing/Chrysalis Music

14 NATURE
THE FOURMYULA
(Mason)
EMI Music Publishing Australia Pty Ltd

15 DRIVE
BIC RUNGA
(Runga)
Warner Chappell Music Australia Pty Ltd

19 VENUS
THE FEELERS
(Reid)
Mushroom Music Publishing

16 SLICE OF HEAVEN
DAVE DOBBYN & HERBS
(Dobbyn)
Mushroom Music Publishing

20 FOR TODAY
NETHERWORLD DANCING TOYS
(Black/Sampson)
Control

21 BETTER BE HOME SOON
CROWDED HOUSE
(Finn)
Mushroom Music Publishing

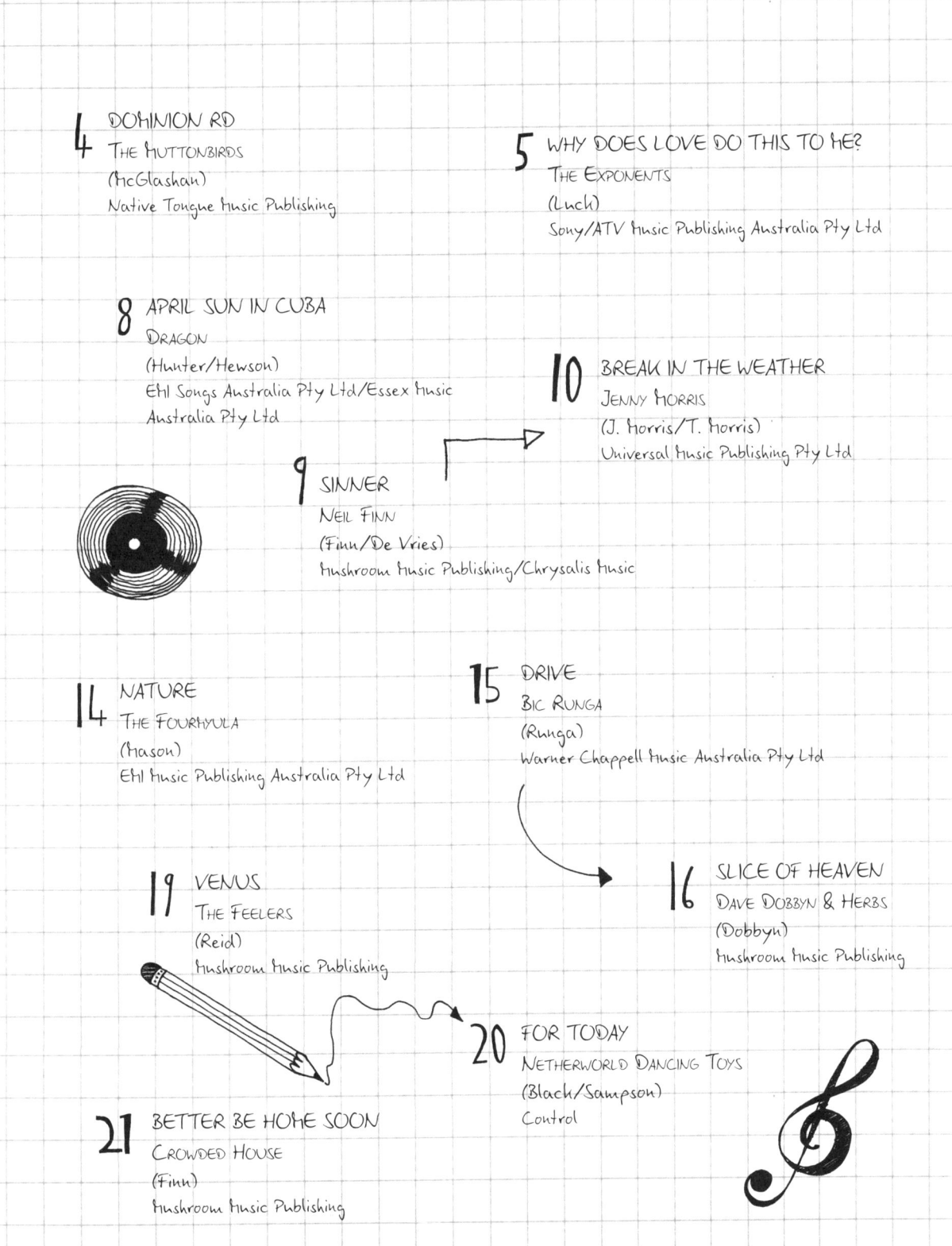

THIS CENTURY

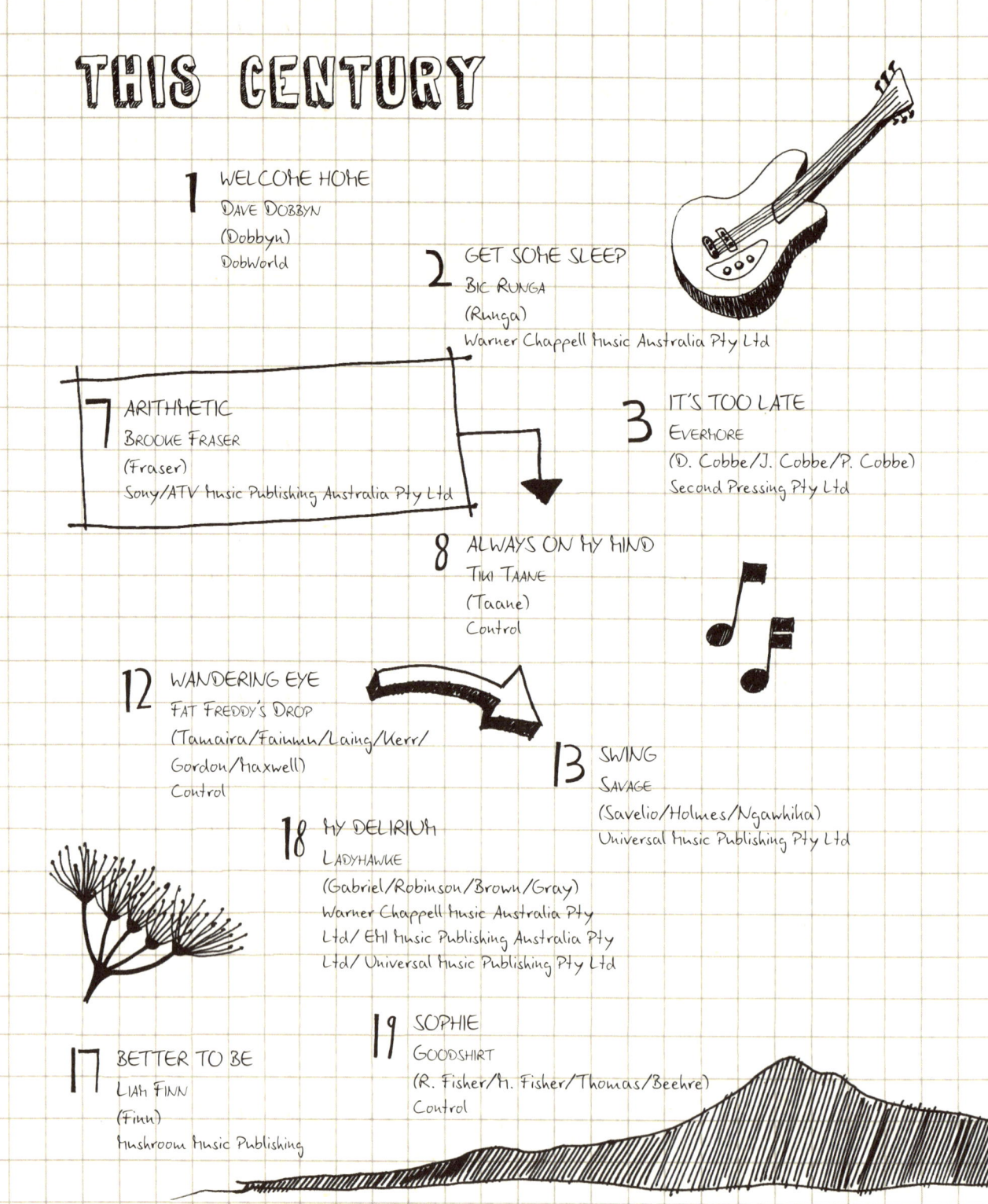

1 WELCOME HOME
DAVE DOBBYN
(Dobbyn)
DobWorld

2 GET SOME SLEEP
BIC RUNGA
(Runga)
Warner Chappell Music Australia Pty Ltd

7 ARITHMETIC
BROOKE FRASER
(Fraser)
Sony/ATV Music Publishing Australia Pty Ltd

3 IT'S TOO LATE
EVERMORE
(D. Cobbe/J. Cobbe/P. Cobbe)
Second Pressing Pty Ltd

8 ALWAYS ON MY MIND
TIKI TAANE
(Taane)
Control

12 WANDERING EYE
FAT FREDDY'S DROP
(Tamaira/Fainmu/Laing/Kerr/
Gordon/Maxwell)
Control

13 SWING
SAVAGE
(Savelio/Holmes/Ngawhika)
Universal Music Publishing Pty Ltd

18 MY DELIRIUM
LADYHAWKE
(Gabriel/Robinson/Brown/Gray)
Warner Chappell Music Australia Pty
Ltd/ EMI Music Publishing Australia Pty
Ltd/ Universal Music Publishing Pty Ltd

19 SOPHIE
GOODSHIRT
(R. Fisher/M. Fisher/Thomas/Beehre)
Control

17 BETTER TO BE
LIAM FINN
(Finn)
Mushroom Music Publishing

5 DAHN THE RIVER
THE PHOENIX FOUNDATION
(Buda/Scott/Wedde/Ricketts/
Singleton/Emery)
Control

4 NO ORDINARY THING
OPSHOP
(Kerrison/Munro/Shedden/
Kennedy/Treacy)
Control

6 COOL ME DOWN
THE BLACK SEEDS
(August/Jaray/McKenzie/Murphy/
Olsen/Weetman)
Native Tongue Music Publishing

9 FOR A WHILE
STELLAR*
(Runga)
Mushroom Music Publishing

11 BATHE IN THE RIVER
HOLLIE SMITH
(McGlashan)
Native Tongue Music Publishing

10 NOT MANY
SCRIBE
(Wadams/Luafutu)
Mushroom Music Publishing

15 OUT OF THIS WORLD
TIM FINN
(Finn)
Mushroom Music Publishing

14 DREAMS IN MY HEAD
ANIKA MOA
(Moa)
Mushroom Music Publishing

16 MAYBE TOMORROW
GOLDENHORSE
(Maddoch)
Native Tongue Music Publishing

20 HOME
Annah Mac
(MacDonald)
Control

21 POKAREKARE ANA
MARGARET URLICH
(Trad.)
AMCOS

THE GREAT NEW ZEALAND SONGBOOK

WHO LOVES WHO THE MOST

PRODUCERS: Murray Thom and Tim Harper

EXECUTIVE PRODUCER: Murray Thom

www.thommusic.com

www.greatnewzealandsongbook.com

THANKS: Steve Anderson, Callum August, John Barnett, Lorraine Barry, Don Bartley, Malcolm Black, Toni Brandso, Brotha D, Chris Caddick, Mike Chunn, Greg Clarke, Martyn Cobbe, Rosie Condon, Julia Connolly, Tony Cowper, Murray Cullen, Tom Dalton, Kevin Denholm, Jackie Dennis, Mary Dobbyn, Morgan Donaghue, Nicole Duckworth, Josh Frizzell, Kirstene Fuemana, Linda Gollan, George Gorga, Chris Gough, Liv Harper, Matt Hawkes, Ant Healey, Emma Hepburn, Grant Hislop, Adam Holt, Phil Howling, Jonathan Hughes, Michelle Jensen, Al Keating, Roger King, Gary Langsford, Alison McLean, Matt McLeod, Tracy Magan, Scott Muir, Andy Murnane, Kelvin Napier, Matt Noonan, Mike Ogle, Teresa Patterson, Janina Percival, Perry Family, Eddie Rayner, Campbell Smith, Brendan Smyth, Maarten van de Vorst, Darryl Ward, Dan Wrightson.

SPECIAL THANKS: The team at Sony Music: Micheal Bradshaw, Noel Barkley, Kim Boshier, Nicky Harrop, Rodney Hewson, Tracey Howard, Scott Morrison, Darryl Parker, Fiona Perry, and Cameron Young. The team at Thom Music: Sarah Cropp, Wendy Nixon, Garry Phipps, Anne Thom and Mary Wells.

COVER ART: Dick Frizzell.

ART DIRECTION AND DESIGN: Tim Harper at Thom Music, with grateful thanks to the artists and songwriters for their co-operation and enthusiasm in sharing their mementos, photos, sketches and paintings, and for hand-writing their lyrics and stories.

PHOTO FINISHING & LAYOUT: Caren Hastings.

PHOTOGRAPHY: "Dominion Road" - Kerry Brown; "Moana Maniapoto" - Andrew Coffey; "No Ordinary Thing" - Steve Dykes; "Rangitoto", "Better Be Home Soon" and "Tihore Mai" - Caren Hastings; "Dave Dobbyn" - Tom Roberton.

PAINTINGS: "My Delirium" - Sarah Larnach watercolour; "Heavenly Pop Hit" - adapted from "The Adoration of the Shepherds, French School" by Annibale Carracci; "Drive" - adapted from an original watercolour by Richard Shaw; "Damn The River" - Jacob Walker watercolour; "Who Loves Who The Most" - Otis Frizzell and Jordan Luck, with thanks to Adam Holt.

ILLUSTRATIONS: "Maybe Tomorrow" - F. Barnard and Harry Furniss, from the book "Beyond The Looking Glass - Extraordinary Works of Fairy Tale & Fantasy", Hart-Davis MacGibbon, London © 1973 Stonehill Publishing Co; "Slice of Heaven" - Murray Ball, courtesy of South Pacific Pictures.

Photographs, paintings, illustrations and articles provided by and used with the kind permission of the artists and songwriters.

Lyrics kindly reproduced courtesy of the publishers.

THIS CENTURY

Welcome Home - DAVE DOBBYN
Get Some Sleep - BIC RUNGA
It's Too Late - EVERMORE
No Ordinary Thing - OPSHOP
Damn the River - THE PHOENIX FOUNDATION
Cool Me Down - THE BLACK SEEDS
Arithmetic - BROOKE FRASER
Always on My Mind - TIKI TAANE
For A while - STELLAR*
Not Many - SCRIBE
Bathe in The River - HOLLIE SMITH
Wandering Eye - FAT FREDDY'S DROP
Swing - SAVAGE
Dreams In My Head - ANIKA w/oA
Out of This World - TIM FINN
Maybe Tomorrow - GOLDENHORSE
Better to Be - LIAM FINN
My Delirium - LADYHAWKE

Sophie - GOODSHIRT
Home - ANNA MACDONALD
Pokarekare Ana - MARGARET URLICH